VALUES IN A TIME
OF UPHEAVAL

VALUES in a TIME of UPHEAVAL

JOSEPH CARDINAL RATZINGER
(POPE BENEDICT XVI)

Translated by Brian McNeil

A Crossroad Book
The Crossroad Publishing Company
New York

Ignatius Press   San Francisco

The Crossroad Publishing Company
16 Penn Plaza – 481 Eighth Avenue, Suite 1550
New York, NY 10001

Originally published as *Werte in Zeiten des Umbruchs: Die Herausforderungen der Zukunft bestehen*, copyright © 2004 by Libreria Editrice Vaticana

Original German edition: copyright © 2005 Verlag Herder, Freiburg im Breisgau, 2 Auflage 2005

English-language edition published by Crossroad Publishing Company and Ignatius Press

Printed in the United States of America

The text of this book is set in 10.5/13.5 Sabon.

Crossroad edition: ISBN 10: 0-8245-2373-3
             ISBN 13: 978-0-8245-2373-2

Ignatius Press edition: ISBN 13: 978-1-58617-140-7
             ISBN 10: 1-58617-140-2
             Library of Congress Control Number 2005933381

1   2   3   4   5   6   7   8   9   10   10   09   08   07   06

Contents

Part III
WHAT IS EUROPE?
Foundations and Perspectives

Preface

❧

Europe has once again become one of the great topics in the public debate about our present and our future. The struggle to elaborate a European constitution, the eastward expansion of the European Union, the question of whether Turkey (a state conscious throughout its history of being a counterfoil to Christian Europe, thanks to its own cultural and religious foundations) should be accepted as a member — all these issues confront us with fundamental questions. What are in fact the foundations on which we live? What supports our societies and holds them together? How do states discern their moral bases and, consequently, also the forces that motivate them to moral conduct — forces without which a state cannot exist? How do we locate ourselves and Europe in the global situation — in the tension between North and South, in the tension between the great cultures of humanity, or in the tension between a technological-secular civilization and those ultimate questions to which it can offer no answer?

These questions took on a new form with the fall of the Berlin Wall in 1989. In the years since then, I have often been invited to lecture and take part in discussions on these subjects. The essays in this book were written in response to these invitations and deal with a variety of themes; I hope that they may form a mosaic that points to the direction to take. Much in this book is a mere sketch, more question than answer. But perhaps it is precisely the incomplete character of these essays that may provide a spur to further thinking on these subjects. I am grateful to Dr. Rudolf Walter of the Herder publishing house for suggesting the collection of these texts. The order of the essays and the overall structure in which they are presented here is the work of the publisher.

JOSEPH CARDINAL RATZINGER

Rome
January 15, 2005

PART

I

WHAT RULES SHOULD
GUIDE OUR CONDUCT?

Politics and Morality

❧

1

To Change or to Preserve?

Political Visions and Political Praxis

❦

Politicians of all parties take it for granted today that they must promise changes — naturally, changes for the better. The once mythical radiance of the word "revolution" has faded in our days, but far-reaching reforms are demanded and promised all the more insistently. This must surely mean that there exists in modern society a deep and prevailing sense of dissatisfaction precisely in those places where prosperity and freedom have attained hitherto unknown heights. The world is experienced as hard to bear. It must become better. And it seems that the task of politics is to bring this about. So since the general consensus is that the essential task of politics is to improve the world, indeed to usher in a new world, it is easy to understand why the word "conservative" has become disreputable and why scarcely anyone views lightly the prospect of being called conservative, for it appears that what we must do is not preserve the status quo but overcome it.

TWO VISIONS OF THE POLITICAL TASK: THE TRANSFORMATION OF THE WORLD OR THE PRESERVATION OF ITS ORDER

This fundamental orientation in the modern conception of politics (indeed, of life in general) is in clear contrast to the views of earlier periods, which considered the great task of political activity to be precisely the preservation and defense of the existing order, warding off threats against it. Here, a small linguistic observation may shed light on this matter.

When Christians in the Roman world were looking for a word that could express succinctly and comprehensibly what Jesus Christ meant to them, they discounted the phrase *conservator mundi* ("conserver of the world"), used in Rome to indicate the essential task and highest service performed in human society. The Christians could not apply this exact title to their Redeemer, nor did they wish to do so, since it was inappropriate as a translation of the words "Messiah/Christ" or as a designation of the Savior of the world. From the perspective of the Roman Empire, the preservation of the ordered structure of the empire against all dangers from within and without had to necessarily be regarded as the most important task of all, because this empire embodied a sphere of peace and law in which it was possible for people to live in security and dignity. And, as a matter of fact, Christians — even as early as the apostolic generation — were aware of the high value of this guarantee of law and peace that the Roman Empire gave them. In view of the looming chaos heralded by the mass migration of peoples, the Church Fathers too were most certainly interested in the survival of the empire, its legal guarantees, and its peaceful order.

Nevertheless, Christians could not simply want everything to remain exactly as it was. The book of Revelation, which certainly stands on the periphery of the New Testament with its view of the empire, nevertheless made it clear to everyone that there were things that must not be preserved, things that had to be changed. When Christ was called *salvator* rather than *conservator*, this had nothing to do with revolutionary political ideas. Yet it did point to the limitations of a mere praxis of preservation and showed a dimension of human existence that went beyond the political functions of maintaining peace and social order.

Let us attempt to move from this snapshot of one way of understanding the essential task of politics onto a rather more fundamental level. Behind the alternative that we have glimpsed somewhat unclearly in the antithesis between the titles *conservator* and *salvator*, we can in fact discern two different visions of what political and ethical conduct can and ought to do. Here it is not only the relationship between politics and morality that is viewed differently but also the interlocking of politics, religion, and morality.

On the one hand, we have the static vision that aims to conserve. It is seen perhaps most clearly in the Chinese understanding of the universe: the ordering of heaven, which always remains the same, prescribes the standards for behavior on earth too. This is the Tao, the law of existence and reality that human beings must recognize and that must govern their conduct. The Tao is both a cosmic and an ethical law. It guarantees the harmony between heaven and earth and, thus, also harmony in political and social life. Disorder, the disturbance of peace, and chaos arise where people resist the Tao, living in disregard of it or even opposition to it. In response to such disturbances and destructions of societal life, the Tao must be reestablished so that the world can once again be livable. The vital issue is to remain aware of the constant ordering of things or to return to it if it has been abandoned.

The Indian concept of *dharma* expresses something similar. This term designates cosmic as well as ethical and social ordering to which human beings must adapt if life is to be led aright. Buddhism relativized this vision — which is at the same time cosmic, political, and religious — by declaring the entire world to be a cycle of suffering; salvation is not to be sought in the cosmos but by departing from it. But Buddhism did not create any new political vision, since the endeavor to attain salvation is nonworldly, orientated to nirvana. No new models are proposed for the world as such.

The faith of Israel takes a different path. In the covenant with Noah it does indeed recognize something akin to a cosmic ordering and the promise that this will be maintained. But for the faith of Israel itself, the orientation to the future becomes ever clearer. It is not that which abides perpetually, a "today" that is always the same, that is seen as the sphere of salvation, but rather a "tomorrow," the future that has not yet arrived. The book of Daniel, probably written in the course of the second century before Christ, presents two great theological visions of history that were to play a very significant role in the further development of political and religious thinking. In the second chapter, we have the vision of the statue that is part gold, part silver, part iron, and, finally, part clay. These four elements symbolize a succession of four kingdoms, all of which are ultimately crushed by a stone that, untouched by human hands, breaks off from a mountain and grinds everything completely to dust so that the wind carries off all that remains, and no trace of the kingdoms can be found. The stone now becomes a high mountain and fills all the earth — the symbol of a kingdom that the God of heaven and earth will establish and that will never pass away (2:44). In the seventh chapter of the same book, the sequence of the kingdoms is depicted in a perhaps even more impressive image as the succession of four animals who are finally judged by God, portrayed as the "Ancient of Days." The four animals — the four mighty empires of world history — had emerged from the sea, which is a metaphor for the power of death to pose a forceful threat to life. But after the judgment comes the human being (the "son of man") from heaven, to whom all peoples, nations, and languages will be handed over to form a kingdom that is eternal and imperishable, never to pass.

While the eternal orderings of the cosmos play a role in the conceptions of the Tao and dharma, the idea of "history" is wholly absent. In the here and now, however, "history" is perceived as a genuine reality that is not reducible to the cosmos. With this anthropological and dynamic reality, which had never been glimpsed in an earlier period, "history" offers a completely different vision. It is clear that such an idea of a historical sequence of kingdoms as gluttonous animals in more and more terrible forms could not have developed in one of the dominant peoples. Rather, it presupposes for its sociological driving force a people that is itself threatened by the greed of these animals and that has also experienced a succession of powers that called into question its very right to existence. This vision belongs to the oppressed, who are on the lookout for a turning point in history and cannot have any desire for the preservation of the status quo. In Daniel's vision, the turning point of history is not the work of political or military activity, for the quite simple reason that the human forces necessary for the task do not exist. It is only through God's intervention that things are changed: the stone that destroys the kingdoms is detached from a mountain "by no human hand" (2:34). The Church Fathers read this as a mysterious prediction of the birth of Jesus from the Virgin, which was the work of God's power alone. In Christ they see the stone that ultimately becomes a mountain and fills the whole earth.

The cosmic visions simply see the Tao or dharma as the power of the divine, as the "divine" itself. But the new element now is not only the appearance of the reality of a "history" that is not reducible to the cosmos, but also this third element — which is also the first, namely, an active God in whom the oppressed put their hope. We see as early as the books of Maccabees, roughly datable to the same period as Daniel's visions, that the human person must also take God's cause into his own hand by means of political and military action. In parts of the Qumran literature the merging of theological hope and human action becomes even clearer. Later on, the struggle of Bar Kochba signifies an unambiguous politicization of messianism: to bring about the turning point in history, God makes use of a "messiah" whom he commissions and empowers to bring in the new order of things by means of active political and military conduct. The "sacred empire" of the Christians, in both its Byzantine and its Latin variants, could not adopt such ideas, nor did it wish to do so. Rather, the primary aim was, again, the preservation of the order of the world, now explained in Christian terms. At the same time, they believed that they were now living in the sixth age of the world, its old age, and that one day the other world would come. This, God's eighth day, was already running alongside history and would one day definitively replace it.

THE REBIRTH OF APOCALYPTICISM IN THE NINETEENTH CENTURY

Apocalypticism — with its refusal to accept the dominant powers of the world and its hope for healing through the overthrow of those powers — never disappeared completely. It reemerged, independent from religion or in opposition to it, from the eighteenth century onward. We encounter its radical form in Marxism, which can be said to follow Daniel to the extent that it offers a negative evaluation of all previous history as a story of oppression and presupposes as its sociological subjects the class of the exploited, both the industrial workers who long enjoyed very few rights and the dependent agricultural laborers. In a remarkable transposition, the reasons for which have not yet been sufficiently reflected on, Marxism became increasingly the religion of the intellectuals, while reforms gave the workers rights that made revolution — that great breaking away from the contemporary form of history — irrelevant. Workers no longer needed the stone that would destroy the kingdoms; they set their hopes rather on Daniel's other image, that of the lion that was set upright on its feet like a human being and received a human heart (7:4). Reform replaced revolution: if the lion has been given a human heart and has laid aside its feral character, then one can live with it. In the world of the intellectuals, most of whom were well off, the rejection of reform became all the louder, and revolution increasingly took on a divine quality. They demanded something completely new; reality as it was evoked a strange feeling of surfeit (and here too we might profitably reflect on the reasons for this feeling).

After all the disappointments prompted in recent years by the collapse of "real socialism," positivism and relativism have now undeniably gained the upper hand. In place of utopian dreams and ideals, today we find a pragmatism that is determined to extract from the world the maximum satisfaction possible. This, however, does not make it pointless to consider once again the characteristics of the secular messianism that appeared on the world stage in Marxism, because it still leads a ghostly existence deep in the souls of many people, and it has the potential to emerge again and again in new forms.

The foundation of this new conception of history rests, on the one hand, on the doctrine of evolution, transferred to the historical sphere, and, on the other hand (linked with that), on a Hegelian belief in progress. The connection to the doctrine of evolution means that history is seen in biologic, indeed in materialistic and deterministic terms: it has its laws and its course, which can be resisted but not ultimately thwarted. Evolution has replaced God here. "God" now means development, progress. But this progress — here Hegel makes his appearance — is realized in dialectical changes; in the last analysis, it too is understood in deterministic terms. The final dialectical move is the leap from the history of oppression into the definitive history of salvation — to employ Daniel's language, we might call this the step from the animals to the "son of man."

The kingdom of the "son of man" is now called the "classless society." Although the dialectical leaps occur of necessity, like events in nature, they are made concrete through political means. The political equivalent to the dialectical leap is revolution, which is a concept antithetical to that of reform. One must reject the idea of reform, because it suggests that the animal has been given a human heart, and one need no longer fight against it. Reforms destroy revolutionary enthusiasm, and this is why they are opposed to the inherent logic of history. They are "involution" instead of evolution and, hence, ultimately the enemies of progress. Revolution and utopia — the anticipation that reaches out to grasp the perfect world — belong together. They are the concrete form taken by this new political and secular messianism. The future is an idol that devours the present; revolution is an idol that obstructs all rational political activity aimed at the genuine amelioration of the world. The theological vision of Daniel, indeed of apocalypticism in general, has been transmuted into something at once secular and mythical, since these two fundamental political ideas — revolution and utopia — present a thoroughly antirational myth when they are combined with evolution and dialectics. Demythologization is urgently needed so that politics can carry on its business in a genuinely rational way.

The Position Taken by the New Testament Writings

In relation to the perspective of Daniel and of political messianisms, what position is taken by Christian faith? What is its vision of history, or its vision for our historical activity? Before I attempt to formulate a brief evaluation, we must look at the most important texts in the New Testament.

No great analytical gifts are required to distinguish two groups of texts. On the one hand, we have the texts of the Gospels and the Acts of the Apostles, which display the most distant connections with apocalypticism. On the other hand, we have the Revelation of John, which — as its very name,

Apokalypsis, shows — belongs to the apocalyptic trajectory. It is well known that the texts of the apostolic letters, in agreement with the view proposed in the Gospels, are utterly free from any trace of revolutionary fervor. Indeed, they are clearly opposed to this: the two fundamental texts, Romans 13:1–6 and 1 Peter 2:13–17, are completely unambiguous, and this has made them offensive to all revolutionaries. Romans 13 demands that everyone (literally, "every soul") submit to the existing authorities, since "there is no authority except from God." This makes resistance to worldly authority a resistance to something God has ordained. Hence, it is not only because of external coercion that one must submit but also "for the sake of one's conscience." In very similar terms, 1 Peter demands submission to the legitimate authorities "for the Lord's sake.... For it is God's will that by doing right you should put to silence the ignorance of foolish men. Live as free men, yet without using your freedom as a pretext for evil." Neither Paul nor Peter expresses an uncritical glorification of the Roman state. While they do insist strongly on the divine origin of the legal ordering of the state, they are far from divinizing the state itself. It is precisely because they see the limits on the state, which is not God and may not behave as if it were God, that they acknowledge its ordering function and its ethical character.

These texts are in a good biblical tradition. We may think here of Jeremiah, who exhorts the exiled Israelites to be loyal to the state of Babylon, which is their oppressor, since this state guarantees law and peace and, thereby, also the relative welfare of Israel — a welfare that is necessary if it is one day to be restored as a people. We may think of Second Isaiah, who does not disdain to call Cyrus God's "anointed." The king of the Persians, who does not know the God of Israel and who is prompted by purely pragmatic political considerations when he sends the people back to their native land, is acting as God's instrument, since he is endeavoring to establish the correct state of affairs. It is on these lines that Jesus answers the Pharisees and the Herodians when they pose the controversial question of paying taxes: "Render to Caesar the things that are Caesar's" (Mark 12:13–17). Since the Roman emperor is the guarantor of law, he has a claim to obedience, though of course Jesus at once specifies the boundaries of the sphere in which one is obliged to obey: there are things that belong to Caesar and things that belong to God. If the emperor exalts himself to a divine position, he has gone beyond his proper limits, and obedience would then amount to a denial of God. Finally, Jesus' reply to Pilate belongs here too. The Lord acknowledges in his words to this unjust judge that the authority to exercise the judicial office, which is at the service of the law, can be bestowed only from above (John 19:11).

Our overview of these texts shows that they hold a very sober view of the state. The personal faith or the subjective good intentions of the organs of the state are not what count. To the extent that they guarantee peace and the rule of law they are in accordance with divine ordinance. In today's terminology, we would say that they represent an ordinance of Creation. It is precisely in its profane character that the state must be respected; it is required by the fact that man is essentially a social and political being. This idea has its basis in the essence of man and hence is in keeping with Creation. At the same time, this entails a limitation on the state. The state has its own sphere, within which it must remain; it must respect the higher law of God. The refusal to adore the emperor and the refusal in general to worship the state are on the most fundamental level simply a rejection of the totalitarian state.

This distinction is made with particular clarity in 1 Peter, when the apostle says: "Let none of you suffer as a murderer, or a thief, or a wrongdoer, or a mischief-maker; yet if one suffers as a Christian, let him not be ashamed, but under that

name let him glorify God" (4:15–16). The Christian is ob-
ligated to the legal order of the state, since this is an ethical
ordering. To suffer "as a Christian" is a different matter: where
the state imposes penalties on the Christian simply for being a
Christian, it rules no longer as a preserver of the law but as its
destroyer. And then it is no disgrace to be punished, but rather
an honor. One who suffers in this manner is following Christ
precisely in his suffering. The crucified Christ indicates the
boundaries to the power of the state and shows where its rights
terminate and resistance in the form of suffering becomes a necessity. The faith of the New Testament acknowledges not the
revolutionary but the martyr who recognizes both the authority of the state and also its limits. His resistance consists in
doing everything that serves to promote law and an ordered
life in society, even when this means obeying authorities who
are indifferent or hostile to his faith; but he will not obey when
he is commanded to do what is evil, that is, to oppose the will
of God. His is not the resistance of active force, but the resistance of the one who is willing to suffer for the will of God.
The resistance fighter who dies with his weapon in his hand is
not a martyr in the New Testament sense.

We find the same position when we study other texts of
the New Testament that deal with the problem of the Christian attitude toward the state. Titus 3:1 says, "Remind them
to be submissive to rulers and authorities, to be obedient, to
be ready for any honest work." An especially significant text
is 2 Thessalonians 3:10–12, where the apostle warns against
those who — no doubt under the pretext that as Christians
they were awaiting the return of the Lord — were unwilling
to work or do anything useful. He exhorts them "to do their
work in quietness," for: "If any one will not work, let him
not eat." An excessively enthusiastic eschatology is soberly cut
down to size. An important aspect is also mentioned in 1 Tim-
othy 2:2, where Christians are admonished to pray "for kings

and all who are in high positions, that we may lead a quiet and peaceable life."

Two things are made clear here: First, Christians pray for kings and other persons in authority, but they do not pray to the king. If this text is from Paul himself, it comes from the reign of Nero; if it is dated later, it may be from the reign of Domitian. Both these emperors were tyrants who hated the Christians, and yet Christians pray for the ruler so that he may be able to fulfill his task. Naturally, they refuse to obey him if he makes himself a god. Second, the task of the state is formulated in an exceptionally sober, indeed almost banal, manner: it must ensure peace at home and abroad. As I have said, this may sound somewhat banal, and yet it articulates an essential moral demand: peace at home and abroad is possible only when the fundamental legal rights of the individual and of society are guaranteed.

Let us now attempt to see how these biblical affirmations are related to the perspective that we have encountered above. I believe that we can say two things here. We find only indirectly the dynamic view of history held by apocalyptic literature and the messianic hopes. Messianism is fundamentally modified by the figure of Jesus. It remains politically relevant, because it marks the point at which martyrdom becomes necessary and a limit is set to the claims that the state is entitled to make. Every martyrdom, however, is subject to the promise made by the risen Christ, who will come again in glory, and this means that martyrdom points beyond the existing world to a new, definitive fellowship that men will enjoy with God and with one another. This limitation of the power of the state and the opening of the horizon onto a future new world do not, however, abolish the existing order of the state, which must continue to govern on the basis of natural reason and of its own logic. This order is valid as long as history lasts. The enthusiastic messianism of an eschatological and revolutionary character is absolutely foreign to the New Testament.

History is, so to speak, the kingdom where reason rules. Although politics does not bring about the kingdom of God, it must be concerned for the right kingdom of human beings, that is, it must create the preconditions for peace at home and abroad and for a rule of law that will permit everyone to "lead a quiet and peaceable life, godly and respectful in every way" (1 Tim. 2:2). One could say that this also implies the demand of religious freedom. Similarly, the text is confident that reason can recognize the essential moral foundations of human existence and can implement these in the political domain. Here we see a point of contact with the positions that declare the Tao or dharma to be the foundation of the state, and this made it possible for Christians to adopt the Stoic idea of an ethical natural law, which won acceptance for similar ideas in the context of Greek philosophy. The dynamic quality attributed to history that becomes particularly visible in the book of Daniel does not see history in simple cosmic terms but interprets it as a dynamic of good and evil in an advancing movement. This remains present, thanks to the messianic hope. It clarifies the ethical criteria of politics and indicates the boundaries of political power. Through the horizon of hope, which it makes visible both beyond and in history, it gives the courage needed for right action and for right suffering. Thus we can speak here of a synthesis of the cosmic and the historical view.

I believe that this allows us to make a precise definition of the boundary between Christian apocalypticism and non-Christian, gnostic apocalypticism. Apocalypticism is Christian if it preserves the connection with Creation faith. Where Creation faith, with its consistency and its trust in reason, is abandoned, Christian faith is transformed into gnosis. Given this fundamental decision, we no doubt find a vast spectrum of variations, but the basic option is the same. I cannot offer an analysis of all the texts of the Revelation of John here, but I would argue that although the vigor of its call to resistance differentiates it from the apostolic letters, nevertheless it remains very clearly within the Christian option.

Consequences for Christian-Involvement in Politics

What consequences may we infer from this for the connection between political vision and political praxis today? One might no doubt write an immensely long monograph on this topic, but I do not feel that that is my task. I would like to offer two theses, indicating as briefly as possible how the consequences of what I have written might be translated into action today.

1. Politics is the realm of reason — not of a merely technological, calculating reason, but of moral reason, since the goal of the state, and hence the ultimate goal of all politics, has a moral nature, namely, peace and justice. This means that moral reason (or, perhaps better, the rational insight into what serves justice and peace, i.e., what is moral) must be activated ever anew and defended against anything that might lend obscurity and thus paralyze the capacity for moral insight. One-sided interests form alliances with power and generate myths in various forms that present themselves as the true path to the moral dimension in politics. But in reality, these are blind spots of those who exercise power — and they make other people blind too.

In the twentieth century, we experienced the formation of two great myths with terrible consequences: racism, with its lying promise of salvation, propagated by National Socialism, and the divinization of revolution against the background of dialectical historical evolutionism. In both cases, the primal moral insights of man into good and evil were dismissed. We were told that whatever served the superiority of the race, or anything that served to bring about the future world, was "good," even if the previous insights of mankind would have called it "bad."

After the disappearance of the great ideologies from the world stage, today's political myths are less clearly defined. But even now there exist mythical forms of genuine values that appear credible precisely because their starting point is these values. They are dangerous because they offer a one-sided version of these values in a way that can only be termed mythical. I would say that in people's general consciousness today, there are three dominant values that are presented in a mythical one-sidedness that puts moral reason at risk. These three are progress, science, and freedom.

Progress has always been a word with a mythical ring. It continues to be portrayed insistently as the norm of political activity and of human behavior in general and as their highest moral qualification. Anyone who looks even at only the last hundred years cannot deny that immense progress has been made in medicine, in technology, and in the understanding and harnessing of the forces of nature, and one may hope for further progress. At the same time, however, the ambivalence of this progress is obvious. Progress is beginning to put Creation — the basis of our existence — at risk; it creates inequality among human beings, and it generates ever new threats to the world and humanity. This makes moral controls of progress indispensable. *But what are the criteria here?*

That is the question. In the first place, we must recognize that progress concerns the dealings of man with the material world. As such, it does not bring forth the new man or the new society, as Marxism and liberalism taught. Man, precisely as man, remains the same both in primitive and in technologically developed situations. He does not stand on a higher level merely because he has learned to use more highly developed tools. Mankind begins anew in every single individual. This is why it is not possible for the definitively new, ideal society to exist — that society built on progress, which not only was the hope of the great ideologies, but increasingly became the general object of human hope once hope in a life after death had been dismantled. A definitively ideal society presupposes the end of freedom. But since man always remains free and begins anew in every generation, we have to struggle in each new situation to establish the right societal form. This is why the realm of politics is concerned with the present, not with the future. It touches on the future only to the extent that today's politics attempts to create forms of law and of peace that can also survive tomorrow and will invite people to similar new elaborations that pick up and carry on the achievements that have been made. But we cannot guarantee this. I believe that it is essential to call to mind these limits on progress and to close the door to a false escape into the future.

The second concept I would like to mention here is *science*. Science is an immensely good thing precisely because it is a controlled form of rationality that is confirmed by experience. But there exist also pathological forms of science that deprive man of all honor, when scientific capabilities are put at the service of power. Science can also serve inhumanity! Here we may recall the weapons of mass destruction, medical experiments on human beings, or the treatment of a person merely as a store of usable organs. Accordingly, it must be clear that science too is subject to moral criteria and that its true nature is lost wherever the only criterion to which it adheres is power or commerce — or even merely success — instead of human dignity.

Third, we have the concept of *freedom*. It too has often taken on mythical traits in the modern period. Freedom is often thought of as something anarchical, something simply opposed to institutions. This makes it an idol, since human freedom can never be anything other than a freedom expressed in the right way of living in common — freedom in justice. Otherwise, it becomes a lie and leads to slavery.

2. We are continually obliged to undertake new demythologizing in order that reason may truly come into its own. Yet here again is another myth that must be unmasked, one that confronts us with the ultimately decisive question of rational politics. In many cases, perhaps in virtually all cases, a majority decision is the "most rational" way to achieve common solutions. But the majority cannot be an ultimate principle, since there are values that no majority is entitled to annul. It can never be right to kill innocent persons, and no power can make this legitimate. Here too, what is ultimately at stake is the defense of reason. Reason — that is, moral reason — is above the majority. But how is it possible to discern these ultimate values that are the basis of all "rational" and morally correct politics and are therefore binding on every person, irrespective of how majorities may shift and change? What are these values?

Constitutional theory in classical antiquity, in the Middle Ages, and even in the conflicts of the modern period, has appealed to the natural law that can be known by "right reason" (*ratio recta*). Today, however, this "right reason" seems to have ceased delivering answers to our questions, and natural law is considered no longer as accessible to the insight of all persons, but rather as a specifically Catholic doctrine. This signifies *a crisis of political reason, which is a crisis of politics as such.* It seems that all that exists today is partisan reason, no longer a reason common to all men, at least as far as the great fundamental structures of values are concerned. All who bear responsibility for peace and justice in the world — and in the last analysis, that means all of us — have the urgent task of working to overcome this state of affairs. This endeavor is by no means hopeless, since reason itself will always make its voice heard against the abuse of power and one-sided partisanship.

There exists today an altered canon of values, which in practice is not called into question but which remains too imprecise and has its blind spots. The triad "peace, justice, and preservation of Creation" is universally recognized, but its contents remain completely vague. What serves the cause of peace? What is justice? How are we to preserve Creation in the best possible way? Other values acknowledged by virtually everyone are the equality of men regardless of race, the equal dignity of the sexes, and freedom of thought and belief. Here, too, the substance of these values is not always clear, and this could come to pose a threat to the freedom of thought and faith. Nevertheless, the fundamental tendencies here are important and deserve our approval.

One essential point remains controversial, namely, the right to life for every person, the inviolability of human life in all its phases. In the name of freedom and in the name of science, increasingly serious holes are being torn in this right. Where abortion is considered a right inherent in human freedom, this means that the freedom of one person is given priority over the other's right to life. Where experiments on unborn human beings are demanded in the name of science, the dignity of man is denied and trampled on precisely in those who are most defenseless. It is here that the concepts of freedom and science must be demythologized if we are not to lose the foundations of all law, respect for man and for his dignity.

A second blind spot is the freedom to scorn what other people regard as holy. We can be very grateful that no one in our country can permit himself to mock that which is holy to Jews or Muslims. But many seem to view as one of the basic rights of human freedom the right to pull down from its pedestal what Christians regard as holy and to heap it with ridicule. And there is yet another blind spot: marriage and family no longer seem to be fundamental values of a modern society. It is urgently necessary to fill in the gaps in the list of values that our society appreciates and to demythologize those values that have undergone a mythical distortion.

In my debate with the philosopher Arcais de Flores, we touched precisely on this point: the limitations of the principle of consensus. The philosopher could not deny that there exist values that even a majority must simply accept. But what are these values? Confronted with this problem, the moderator of the debate, Gad Lerner, asked, "Why not take the Ten Commandments as a criterion?" It is perfectly correct to point out that the Decalogue is not the private property of Christians or Jews: it is a sublime expression of moral reason, and as such it finds echoes in the wisdom of the other great cultures. To take the Ten Commandments as our criterion might be a tremendous help in healing reason so that "right reason" may once again get to work.

This also makes clear what faith can contribute to correct politics. Faith does not make reason superfluous, but it can contribute evidence of essential values. Through the experiment of a life in faith, these values acquire a credibility that also illuminates and heals reason. In the last century (as in every century), it was in fact the testimony of the martyrs that limited the excesses of power, thus making a decisive contribution to what we might call the convalescence of reason.

2

What Keeps the World Together

The Prepolitical Moral Foundations
of a Free State

೮ఢ

Developments that began slowly in the past have speeded up
immensely in our own days, and I believe that the current
historical situation is characterized above all by two factors.
First, there is the formation of a global society in which the
individual political, economic, and cultural forces are increasingly interrelated. In their various realms they intersect and
influence one another. Second, the development of man's power
to create and to destroy poses much more acutely than before
the question of the legal and ethical controls on this power. It
is therefore imperative, in the encounter of various cultures, to
identify ethical bases that can point out the right way for them
to live and work together and enable them to set up cooperative
structures for controlling and regulating the exercise of power.

The fact that the project of a "world ethos," proposed
by Hans Küng, finds such an echo demonstrates at the very
least that he has posed a serious question, even if one accepts
the sharp criticisms that Robert Spaemann has made of this
project.[1]

---

1. R. Spaemann, "Weltethos als 'Projekt,'" *Merkur*, nos. 570/571, pp. 893–
904.

We must also take a third factor into account: in the process whereby the cultures encounter and influence one another, ethical certainties that were the foundation of society in the past have broken down. The basic question of what is good, and why one should do what is good even where this is to one's own disadvantage, remains largely unanswered in the public domain.

It is seems to me obvious that science per se cannot generate any ethics and that therefore a renewed ethical consciousness does not emerge as the product of academic debates. On the other hand, it is also indisputable that the fundamental transformation of the image of the world and of man as a result of increasing scientific knowledge is an essential contributor to the dissolution of old moral certainties. This means that science does have a responsibility in terms of man *qua* man. In particular, philosophy has a responsibility to accompany critically the individual sciences, shedding a critical light on rash inferences and on merely apparent certainties about what man is, where he comes from, and what the purpose of human existence might be. We can express this point as follows: philosophy must detach the nonscientific element from scientific elements with which it is often mixed. Since science can show us individual aspects of the reality of human existence, but never the wider dimensions, it is philosophy's task to help us see the totality.

POWER AND LAW

It is the specific task of politics to subordinate power to the criterion of law, thereby regulating the meaningful use of power. It is not the law of the strongest that must prevail, but rather the strength of the law. The use of power to regulate and serve the law is the opposite pole of a power that knows no law or that flouts the law — and that is a power we call "violence."

This makes it vital for every society to remove everything that could cast suspicion on the law and its ordinances, because it is only in this way that arbitrary conduct on the part of the state can be eliminated and freedom can be experienced as something genuinely shared by all. A freedom without law is anarchy and therefore the destruction of freedom. The law will come under suspicion, and people will revolt against the law, whenever it is perceived, no longer as the expression of a justice that is at the service of all, but rather as a product of despotism, of an arrogance that is clothed in the garments of law by those who have the power to do so.

This task of subordinating power to the criterion of law prompts a further question: How does law arise, and how ought law to be, in order to serve as a vehicle of justice and not simply be the privilege of those who happen to possess the power to make laws? Here we have two questions: the genesis of law, and the criteria inherent in law. The problem that law ought be, not the instrument by means of which a few persons exercise power, but rather the expression of the common interest of all, seems — initially at least — to be resolved by democratic decision making. Since all collaborate in the genesis of the law, it is common to all. As such, all can and must respect it. And as a matter of fact, democracy's guarantee that all can work together to shape the law and the just distribution of power is the fundamental reason why democracy is the most appropriate of all political models.

Nevertheless, I believe that one question remains open. Since absolute unanimity among men is a utopian idea, the only instruments whereby a democracy can make decisions are delegation and majority rule. Depending on the importance of the question, a larger majority than usual may sometimes be demanded. However, even majorities can be blind or unjust. History makes that absolutely clear. Let us suppose that an overwhelming majority oppresses a religious or ethnic minority by means of harsh legislation — would we then speak of "justice," or even of "the rule of law"? The majority principle always leaves open the question of the ethical foundations of law: Are there some things that can never be legalized, some things that always remain wrong? On the other hand, are there some things that absolutely always remain legally binding, things that precede every majority decision, things that majority decisions must respect?

The modern age has formulated a number of such normative elements in its various declarations of human rights. These can not be altered by shifts in parliamentary majorities. Contemporary consciousness may perhaps be content to hold that these values possess a self-evident quality and, thus, ask no further questions. But even such self-limiting of questions has a philosophical character. So there are unconditional values that follow from the essence of what it is to be human, and these must be respected by everyone. We must return below to the extent to which this claim is actually valid, since this evidential quality is not accepted in all cultures. Islam has its own catalogue of human rights, which is not the same as the Western one. And although China is governed today by a cultural form that arose in the West, Marxism, its government appears to hold (if I am informed correctly) that "human rights" are merely a typically Western invention that cannot be accepted without further examination.

NEW FORMS OF POWER AND NEW QUESTIONS ABOUT HOW TO CONTROL THEM

When we discuss the relationship between power and law and the sources of law, we must look more closely at the phenomenon of power itself. I do not wish to attempt to define the essence of "power" as such, but merely to sketch briefly the challenges posed by the new forms of power that have developed in the last fifty years.

The initial period after the Second World War was dominated by the fear of the new destructive power that the invention of the atomic bomb had placed in man's hands. Man suddenly realized that he had the power to destroy himself and his world, and this prompted the questions: What political mechanisms are required in order to prevent such destruction? How are such mechanisms to be identified and made effective? How can we mobilize ethical forces that will create such political forms and make them effective? In fact, we were preserved from the horrors of a nuclear war for a long time by the competition between opposing power blocs and the fear that one would destroy one's own side if one were to initiate the destruction of the other side. The mutual limitation of power, and the fear that one's own side might not survive, proved to be the saving forces.

Today it is not so much fear of a large-scale war that causes us sleepless nights but rather fear of the omnipresent terrorism that can become operative and strike anywhere. We have come to see that mankind does not even need a large-scale war for the world to become utterly inhospitable. The anonymous forces of terrorism, which can be present everywhere in the world, are strong enough to pursue us into our daily lives. The specter remains that criminal elements could get hold of potentially destructive weapons so that forces outside the political sphere could plunge the world into utter chaos. The questions about law and ethics have therefore shifted focus: What are the sources that generate *terror*? How can we succeed in eliminating this new sickness of mankind from within? One frightening thing here is that terror claims to be morally legitimate, at least in part. Osama bin Laden's messages portray terror as the response of the powerless and oppressed peoples to the arrogance of the mighty, as the righteous punishment for their presumption and for their blasphemous high-handedness and cruelty. Men in certain societal and political situations apparently find such motivations convincing. In part terrorism is presented as the defense of religious tradition against the godlessness of Western society.

Here too there is a question to which we must return: If religious fanaticism is one of the sources on which terrorism draws — and it is — *can it be correct to call religion a healing and saving force? Is it not rather an archaic and dangerous force* that constructs false universalisms, thereby leading to intolerance and terror? Must not religion be placed under the guardianship of reason and be strictly circumscribed? This of course prompts further questions: Who can do this? And how is it to be achieved? But the general question remains: Must the gradual disappearance and elimination of religion be considered necessary progress for mankind so that it can begin to take the path of freedom and universal tolerance? Or is this view mistaken?

Another form of power has likewise become prominent. Initially it appears wholly beneficial and worthy of praise, but in reality it too can represent a new kind of threat to man. Man is now capable of making men, of producing them in test tubes, so to speak. Man becomes a product, and this fundamentally alters man's relationship to himself. He is no longer a gift of nature or of the Creator God: he is his own product. Man has climbed down into the wellsprings of power, to the source of his very existence. The temptation now to construct the "correct" man at last, the temptation to experiment with human beings, the temptation to see them as garbage and to get rid of them — this is not some fantastic notion of moralists inimical to progress.

We have already noted the urgent question whether religion is genuinely a positive force. Here, we must face *doubts about the reliability of reason.* For in the last analysis, even the atomic bomb is a product of reason, just as the breeding and selection of human beings in the laboratory have also been thought out by reason. Must we not therefore say that it is reason that needs a guardian? But who or what could perform this task? Ought we perhaps to say that religion and reason should impose limitations on one another, each demarcating the proper sphere of the other and helping it to develop positively?

Once again, we are confronted by the question of how it is possible, in a global society with its mechanisms of power and its unrestrained forces and with its various views of what is law and what is morality, to identify ethical values with a genuinely evidential character — values sufficiently strong to provide motivation and sufficiently capable of being implemented so that they can offer an answer to the challenges I have sketched here and can help us meet them successfully.

Presuppositions of Law:
Law — Nature — Reason

The obvious first step is to look at historical situations comparable to our own. One may perhaps wonder whether such situations exist, but it is surely worth bearing in mind that Greece had its "Enlightenment," as a result of which law (previously based on the gods) lost its evidential character. It was necessary to inquire into deeper grounds for law. So the idea arose that, in view of the fact that existing law ("positive law") may in fact be unjust, there must be a law that derives from nature, from the very existence of man. This law must be identified so that it may act as a corrective to positive law.

We need go no further into the past than the double breach of continuity in European consciousness at the beginning of the modern period that made it necessary to reflect anew on the substance and the source of law. The first factor was the dissolution of the borders of the European and Christian world that occurred when America was discovered. Now European

Christians encountered peoples who did not belong to the ordered structure of faith and of law that had hitherto supplied the source and the form of law for everyone. But did that mean that they were outside the law — as many asserted at that time, with appalling consequences for the way they treated the inhabitants of the Americas? Or is there in fact a law that transcends all legal systems, binding together men as men and constantly reminding them of this deeper unity? In this situation, Francisco de Vitoria elaborated the already existing concept of the *ius gentium*, the "law of the peoples"; the word *gentes* evokes the "Gentiles" or "pagans," the non-Christians. That meant a law antecedent to the forms of Christian law, a law whose task was to regulate the correct mutual relationships of all peoples.

The second breach in continuity in the Christian world took place within Christendom itself through the schism in faith that led to the development of distinct Christian communities that were often hostile to one another. Once again, it proved necessary to elaborate a common law antecedent to dogma, or at least a legal minimum based no longer on Christian faith but on nature, on human reason. Hugo Grotius, Samuel von Pufendorf, and others developed the idea of natural law as a rational law that transcends confessional boundaries and permits reason to work as the instrument whereby a common law may be posited.

Natural law has remained — especially in the Catholic Church — one element in the arsenal of arguments in conversations with secular society and with other communities of faith, appealing to shared reason in the attempt to discern the basis of a consensus about ethical principles of law in a pluralistic, secular society. Unfortunately, this instrument has become blunt, and that is why I do not wish to employ it to support my arguments in this discussion. The idea of the natural law presupposed a concept of "nature" in which nature and reason interlock: nature itself is rational. The victory of the theory of evolution has meant the end of this view of nature. According to this theory, which seems to go broadly unchallenged today, nature per se is not rational, although it does contain rational behavior.[2] The concept of nature on which the former natural law was based had various dimensions; the only one that survives today is the well-known proposition formulated in Ulpian, early in the third century after Christ: *Ius naturae est, quod natura omnia animalia docet* ("The law of nature is that which nature teaches all living beings").[3] But this does not suffice to answer our questions, which do not concern that which is common to all *animalia* but rather envisage specifically human tasks that human reason has created and that cannot be answered without reason.

By natural law, on the deepest level and at least in the modern period, was meant a rational law. Its last surviving element is *human rights*. These are incomprehensible without the presupposition that man as such, in virtue of the simple fact that he belongs to the species "man," is the subject of rights. His

---

2. This philosophy of evolution remains dominant despite some corrections in detail. The most impressive application is by J. Monod, *Chance and Necessity: An Essay on the Natural Philosophy of Modern Biology* (New York, 1971). On the distinction between the de facto results of research in the natural sciences and the philosophy that accompanies them, a helpful book is R. Junker and S. Scherer, eds., *Evolution: Ein kritisches Lehrbuch*, 4th ed. (Giessen, 1998). For reflections on the debate with the philosophy that accompanies the theory of evolution, see J. Ratzinger, *Truth and Tolerance: Christian Belief and World Religions*, trans. Henry Taylor (San Francisco: Ignatius Press, 2004), 162–83.

3. On the three dimensions of the medieval natural law (the dynamic of existence in general; the inherent directional quality of that nature which is common to man and animals [Ulpian]; the specific directional quality of the rational nature of man), see the article by P. Delhaye, "Naturrecht," in *Lexikon für Theologie und Kirche*, 2nd ed., VII, cols. 821–25. We should also note the concept of natural law that stands at the beginning of the *Decretum Gratiani: Humanum genus duobus regitur, naturali videlicet iure, et moribus. Ius naturale est, quod in lege et Evangelio continetur, quo quisque iubetur, alii facere, quod sibi vult fieri, et prohibetur, alii inferre, quod sibi nolit fieri.* ("The human race is governed by two things, viz., the natural law and customs. The natural law is that which is contained in the law and the Gospel, whereby each one is commanded to do to another what he wishes to be done to himself and is forbidden to inflict on another what he does not wish to be done to himself.")

existence bears in itself values and norms that must be discovered but not invented. Perhaps the doctrine of human rights
ought today to be complemented by a doctrine of human obligations and human limits. This might help shed new light on
the question of whether there exists reason inherent in nature,
and hence a rational law applicable to man and to his existence
in the world. Today we would have to conduct the discussion
of these matters in an intercultural context. Christians would
see them as connected with Creation and the Creator. In the
Indian world, they would be connected with the concept of
dharma, the inherent regularity of existence; in the Chinese
tradition, one would find the idea of the regulations laid down
by heaven.

Interculturality and Its Consequences

Before attempting to reach a conclusion, I should like to ex-
pand a little on what I have just said. It seems to me that
interculturality is an indispensable condition today for the discussion of the fundamental questions of human existence. This
debate cannot be carried on by Christians on their own, nor
can it be limited to the Western rational tradition. Both Christianity and the Western rational tradition do in fact understand
themselves to be universal, and it is certainly possible that this
view is correct de jure — but de facto they are obliged to acknowledge that they are accepted by only a part of mankind.
Indeed, they are comprehensible only to a part of mankind, although of course the number of rival cultures is much smaller
than an initial glance might suggest.

   The most important point in our present context is that
there is no longer any uniformity within individual cultural
spheres. Rather, every cultural sphere bears the marks of deep
tensions within its own cultural tradition. This is completely
obvious in the West. Jürgen Habermas has painted an impressive portrait of the strict rationality that is to a large extent

dominant in secular culture and that understands itself as the force that holds that culture together. But the Christian understanding of reality also continues to be a powerful force in the West. The relationship between the two visions of reality is sometimes close and sometimes tense. Sometimes they are willing to learn from each other, and sometimes they wash their hands of each other with a greater or lesser degree of finality.

Similar tensions exist in the Islamic cultural sphere too: there is a broad spectrum from the fanatical absolutism of a bin Laden to attitudes that are open to embrace a tolerant rationality. The third great cultural sphere, that of India — or better, the cultural spheres of Hinduism and Buddhism — have other tensions that may appear less dramatic to our Western eyes. These cultures too are challenged by Western rationality and by the questions posed by Christian faith, both of which are present in India. Buddhism and Hinduism assimilate these challenges in a variety of ways while seeking to preserve their own identity. The tribal cultures of Africa and those of Latin America, which have been reawakened to life by some Christian theologians, complete the picture. They often seem to call Western rationality into question, and they also seem to question the claim of Christian revelation to universal validity.

Where does all this lead us? I believe that the first conclusion is the actual nonuniversality of the two great Western cultures, the culture of Christian faith and the culture of secular rationality, although of course both of these have a powerful influence in the entire world and in every culture, each in its own way. Hence, I believe that the question posed by the philosopher in Teheran whom Jürgen Habermas has mentioned is not unimportant: From the perspective of comparative cultural studies and the sociology of religion, is not European secularization a deviant development that needs to be corrected? I would not necessarily reduce the relevance of this question so that it applied only to the "atmosphere" of Carl Schmitt, Martin Heidegger, and Levi Strauss, i.e., to a European situation that has become weary of rationality.

At any rate, it is a fact that our secular rationality, be it ever so plausible to our own reason (which itself was formed in the West), does not convince every *ratio*. As rationality, it fails in the attempt to demonstrate its evidential character, which is de facto limited to particular cultural contexts. It must acknowledge that it cannot win acceptance as rationality by the whole of mankind and that it cannot operate fully in mankind as a whole. In other words, there is no single rational or ethical or religious "world formula" that could win acceptance by everyone and could then provide support for the whole. At any rate, such a formula is unattainable at present. This is why the so-called "world ethos" remains an abstraction.

Conclusions

What then ought we to do? As far as practical consequences are concerned, I agree broadly with Jürgen Habermas's remarks about a postsecular society, about willingness to learn, and about self-limitation in both directions. I should like to summarize my own viewpoint in two theses and then conclude.

First, we have seen that there exist highly dangerous *pathologies in religion* that make it necessary to regard the divine light of reason as a kind of controlling authority. Religion must continually accept the purification and regulation that reason carries out — and I may note in passing that this was the view of the Church Fathers too.[4] Our considerations have however shown that there also exist no less dangerous *pathologies of reason* (a fact of which people today in general are less aware), a hubris of reason. Indeed, the potential effectiveness of these

---

4. I have attempted to set this out in greater detail in my book *Truth and Tolerance* (see note 2 above); see also M. Fiedrowicz, *Apologie im frühen Christentum*, 2nd ed. (Paderborn, 2001).

pathologies of reason makes them an even greater threat: for example, the atomic bomb and man as a product. This is why reason too must be admonished to keep to its own boundaries and to learn to listen to what the great religious traditions of mankind have to say. If reason becomes fully emancipated and lays aside this willingness to learn, this correlation with religion, it takes on a destructive character.

Kurt Hübner has recently formulated a similar demand, arguing that such a thesis does not directly involve a "return to faith" but insists "that one free oneself from the governing illusion of our age, that is, that faith has nothing more to say to people today because it would entail a contradiction of our modern humanistic idea of reason, enlightenment, and freedom."[5] In keeping with this affirmation, I would speak of a necessary correlation between reason and faith, reason and religion, which are called to purify and heal one another. They need each other, and they must acknowledge one another's validity.

Second, this basic rule must be specified in praxis, in the intercultural context in which we live today. There can be no doubt that the two principal partners in this correlation are Christian faith and Western secular rationality. One can affirm this, and indeed one must affirm it; it does not entail a false Eurocentrism, since these two determine the situation of the world in a way unparalleled by any other cultural forces. But this does not mean that one may push aside other cultures as a kind of *quantité négligeable*, for that would be a Western hubris for which a high price would have to be paid — and we are in fact already paying a part of that price. It is important for the two great components of Western culture to be willing to *listen* and to accept a genuine correlation with these cultures

---

5. K. Hübner, *Das Christentum im Wettstreit der Religionen* (Tübingen, 2003), 148.

also. It is important to include them in the attempt at a poly-
phonic correlation in which these cultures themselves will be
open to learn from the Western complementarity of faith and
reason. This would permit the growth of a universal process
of purification in which those essential values and norms that
are known or at least guessed at by all men could acquire a
new radiance. In this way, that which keeps the world together
would once again become an effective force in mankind.

3

Freedom, Law, and the Good

Moral Principles in Democratic Societies

❧

It is a great honor for me to be appointed a member of the Institut de France, especially as the successor to a great figure like Andrey Dimitriyevich Sakharov. I am profoundly grateful for this. Sakharov was an important physicist, but he was more than a great scientist: he was a great man. For the sake of the humanity of man, of his ethical dignity and his freedom, Sakharov accepted the price of suffering and of persecution; he gave up the possibility of continuing his scientific work. Science can serve humanity, but it can also become an instrument of evil. Indeed, it is science that has the potential to make evil truly terrible. It is only when scientific work is sustained by ethical responsibility that it is able to be what it is meant to be.

THE PUBLIC CLAIM OF CONSCIENCE

I do not know when and how Sakharov came to realize the full seriousness of these facts, but we have one indication in a short note he left about an event in 1955. In November of that year, tragic events occurred when very important experiments with thermonuclear weapons were carried out: a young soldier

45

and a two-year-old girl died. At a small dinner party held after the conclusion of the experiments, Sakharov raised his glass for a toast and remarked that he hoped that Russian weapons would never explode over cities. In his reply, the director of the test, a high-ranking officer, declared that it was the scientist's task to improve the weapons, but it was not up to him to decide how those weapons were employed. The understanding of the scientist as a scientist had no competence in this matter. Sakharov commented that he already believed at that date what he still believed, "that no individual can refuse to shoulder his share of the responsibility for a matter on which the existence of mankind depends."[1] The officer may well not have been aware of the significance of his words, but he was basically denying the existence of the ethical dimension as a reality in which every man is competent. Clearly, he thought that there were only professional competences of a scientific, political, or military nature.

In reality, however, there exists no professional competence that could confer the right to kill people or to allow them to be killed. The denial of a shared human capability to understand that which concerns man as man creates a new class system and thereby degrades everyone, since man as such is no longer permitted to exist. The denial of the ethical principle, the denial of a capacity for insight that is antecedent to every specialization — that capacity for insight which we call "conscience" — is a denial of man. Sakharov insisted again and again, with great urgency, on this responsibility that each individual bears for the totality. He discovered his own mission when he perceived the reality of this responsibility.

After 1968, he was excluded from working on projects that involved state secrets, but he maintained all the more loudly the public claim of conscience. Henceforth, his thinking centered on human rights, on the moral renewal of his

---

1. See A. D. Sakharov, *Mein Land und die Welt*, 2nd ed. (Vienna, 1976), 82.

country and of mankind, on shared human values in general, and on the commandment issued by conscience. He loved his country very deeply, but he was forced to become the accuser of a regime that drove people to apathy, weariness, and indifference, reducing them to external and internal poverty.

One could of course say that the fall of the Communist system has brought Sakharov's mission to an end: it was an important chapter in the history of political morality, but it now belongs to the past. I believe that such a view would be a grave and dangerous error. To begin with, it is clear that Sakharov's general orientation to human dignity and human rights, and his obedience to his conscience even at the price of suffering, constitute an abiding message that does not lose its contemporary relevance merely because of the disappearance of the specific political context that had initially made it relevant.

Besides this, under the rule of the Marxist parties, a number of risks to man took the form of concrete political forces that were destroying the human quality of life, and I believe that these risks continue to exist, albeit in another form.

Robert Spaemann has observed that after the collapse of utopia, a banal nihilism is beginning to spread today, and that its results may be no less insidious.[2] He mentions the example of the American philosopher Richard Rorty, who has formulated the new utopia of banality. Rorty's ideal is a liberal society in which absolute values and criteria will no longer exist; a sense of well-being will be the only goal worth striving for. In his cautious but resolute criticism of the Western world, Sakharov anticipated the danger inherent in this emptying-out of what is human and spoke accordingly of a "left-wing liberal

---

2. R. Spaemann, "La perle précieuse et le nihilisme banal," *Catholica*, no. 33 (1992): 43–50; quotation from 45.

fashion" and attacked the naiveté and cynicism that so frequently paralyze the West precisely when it is vital to perceive its moral responsibility.[3]

INDIVIDUAL FREEDOM
AND COMMUNITY VALUES

Here we see the question that Sakharov addresses to us today: How can the free world do justice to its moral responsibility? Freedom preserves its dignity only as long as it retains the relationship to its ethical foundations and to its ethical task. A freedom that consisted solely in the possibility of satisfying one's needs would not be human freedom, since it would remain in the animal realm. An individual freedom without substance dissolves into meaninglessness, since the individual's freedom can exist only in an order of freedoms. Freedom requires a communal substance, which we could define as the guaranteeing of human rights. We can put this in other terms: the very essence of the concept of "freedom" demands that it be complemented by two other concepts, those of law and of the good. We might say that freedom entails the ability of the conscience to perceive the fundamental value of humanity, a value that concerns every individual.

At this point, we must develop Sakharov's thinking today in order to transpose it appropriately into the contemporary situation. Despite all his gratitude for the intervention of the free world on his behalf and in favor of other victims of Soviet persecution, Sakharov repeatedly experienced the failures of the West in a dramatic fashion, both in many political events and in the personal fates of many individuals. He did not see his task as the analysis of the underlying reasons for these failures, but he did clearly grasp that freedom is often understood in an

---

3. Sakharov, *Mein Land und die Welt*, 17; see also 44f., etc.

egotistic and superficial manner.[4] One cannot desire freedom for oneself alone; freedom is indivisible and must always be seen as a task to be achieved on behalf of mankind as a whole. This means that one cannot have freedom without paying the price of sacrifices and renunciation. Freedom demands that we undertake to understand morality as a public and communal obligation. Morality in itself has no power, but we must recognize that only the moral dimension possesses the true power to promote man. Freedom demands that governments and all those who bear responsibility bow down before a reality that is defenseless and incapable of exercising any coercion: morality.

It is here that the risk to modern democracies lies, and we must confront it in the spirit of Sakharov. For it is hard to see how democracy, which is based on the majority principle, can accord validity to moral values that are not sustained by the conviction of the majority unless it imports a dogmatism that is alien to its own nature. Rorty suggests here that a reason orientated to the majority will always include a number of intuitive ideas such as the rejection of slavery.

P. Bayle expressed an even greater optimism in the seventeenth century. At the close of the bloody wars generated by the terrible conflicts regarding faith in Europe, Bayle affirmed that metaphysics had nothing to do with political life; practical truth was enough. There was only one single, universal, and necessary morality, which was a true and clear light perceived by all men, provided that they opened their eyes.[5] Bayle's ideas reflect the intellectual situation of his century: the unity in faith had crumbled, and it was no longer possible to hang on to truths of the metaphysical sphere as something shared by both Catholics and Protestants. As yet, however, the essential fundamental moral convictions that Christianity had imprinted on people's souls were still certainties taken for granted, and it

---

4. See ibid., 21f., 89.
5. See V. Possenti, *Le società liberali al bivio: Lineamenti di filosofia della società* (Genoa, 1991), 293.

seemed that unaided reason could perceive the pure evidential character of these convictions.

The developments of the twentieth century have taught us that this evidential character — as the subsistent and reliable basis of all freedom — no longer exists. It is perfectly possible for reason to lose sight of essential values. Nor is intuition, on which Rorty bases his system, absolutely reliable. For example, he adduces the insight that slavery is unacceptable; but for centuries, such an insight did not exist at all, and the history of the totalitarian states in the twentieth century demonstrates with sufficient clarity how easy it is to abandon this insight. Freedom can abolish itself. Freedom can weary of itself when it has become empty. The twentieth century has also offered examples of a majority decision that served to abrogate freedom.

Behind Sakharov's unease when he experienced the naiveté and cynicism of the West lies the problem of an empty and directionless positivism. The strict positivism that is expressed in the absolutization of the majority principle is inevitably transmuted at some point into nihilism. If we are to defend freedom and human rights, we must neutralize this risk.

In 1938, the Danzig politician Hermann Rauschning diagnosed National Socialism as a revolution of nihilism: "There has been, and there is now, no goal that National Socialism would not be willing at any time to relinquish, or else to propose, if this action benefited the Movement."[6] National Socialism was merely an instrument employed by nihilism; it was ready to discard this instrument at any time and to replace it by another. It seems to me that the label of "hostility to foreigners" does not quite fit the events that we observe with some unease in today's Germany. Here too there is ultimately a nihilism at work that is the by-product of the emptying of

---

6. H. Rauschning, *Die Revolution des Nihilismus* (Zurich, 1938), new abbreviated edition by Golo Mann, Zurich, 1964. See J. Ratzinger, *Kirche, Ökumene und Politik* (Einsiedeln, 1987), 153f.

souls: neither the Nazi nor the Communist dictatorship considered any specific action in itself as evil and invariably immoral. Whatever served the goals of the Movement or the Party was good, irrespective of how inhuman it might appear. This means that moral sensibility has been trampled on for decades, and this must inevitably turn into a moral nihilism as soon as none of the previous goals counts any longer. All that remained was freedom — but this was understood as the possibility of doing anything and everything that could supply a momentary excitement and interest to a life that had become empty.

RESPECT FOR A BASIC ELEMENT OF HUMANITY

Let us return to the question of how it is possible to strengthen law and the good in our societies so that they can do battle against naiveté and cynicism without imposing the power of law by external coercion or defining it arbitrarily. In this context, de Tocqueville's analysis in *Democracy in America* has always impressed me. This great political thinker saw one essential precondition for the cohesion of this fragile structure, which made possible the regulation of freedoms in a communal experience of freedom. This precondition lay in the vitality in America of a basic moral conviction (nourished by Protestantism) that supplied the foundational structures of institutions and democratic mechanisms,[7] and it is perfectly true that institutions cannot survive and work effectively without shared ethical convictions. These, however, cannot be the product of merely empirical reason. Even majority decisions become truly human and rational only when they presuppose a basic human element that they respect as the real common good that is the presupposition of all other good things. Such convictions demand corresponding human attitudes, but these attitudes

---

7. A. Jardin, *Alexis de Tocqueville 1805–1859* (Paris, 1984), 210.

cannot flourish unless the historical basis of a culture and the ethical-religious insights that it preserves are taken seriously. A culture and a nation that cuts itself off from the great ethical and religious forces of its own history commits suicide. The cultivation of essential moral insights, preserving and protecting these as a common possession but without imposing them by force, seems to be one condition for the continued existence of freedom in the face of all the nihilisms and their totalitarian consequences.

It is here that I see the public task of the Christian churches in today's world. It accords with the nature of the Church that it is separated from the state and that its faith may not be imposed by the state but is based on convictions that are freely arrived at. Origen made a fine comment here, which unfortunately has not received the attention it deserves: "Christ does not win victory over anyone who does not wish it. He conquers only by convincing, for he is the *Word* of God."[8] It is an essential aspect of the Church that it is neither the state nor a part of the state but a *fellowship based on conviction*. But it is also essentially aware of its responsibility for the totality: it cannot accept a limitation to its own affairs. On the basis of its own freedom, it must address the freedom of all human beings so that the moral forces of history may remain forces in the present. This will permit people, in continually changing circumstances, to grasp the evidential character of those values without which a shared freedom is impossible.

---

8. *Fragments on the Psalms* 4:1, PG 12:1133 B; see also M. Geerard, *Clavis Patrum Graecorum* I, 1983, p. 151.

4

What Is Truth?

The Significance of Religious and Ethical Values in a Pluralistic Society

❧

RELATIVISM AS A PRECONDITION OF DEMOCRACY

Since the collapse of the totalitarian systems that left their mark on long stretches of the twentieth century, many people today have become convinced that, even if democracy does not bring about the ideal society, nevertheless it is in practice the only appropriate system of government. It brings about a distribution and control of power, thereby offering the greatest possible guarantee against despotism and oppression and ensuring the freedom of the individual and the maintenance of human rights. When we speak of democracy today, it is above all these good things that we have in mind. The participation of everyone in power is the hallmark of freedom. No one is to be merely the object of rule by others or only a person under control; everyone ought to be able to make a voluntary contribution to the totality of political activity. We can all be free citizens only if we all have a genuine share in decision making.

The real goal of participation in power is thus universal freedom and equality. But since power cannot be continuously exercised in an immediate manner by everyone, it must be delegated for a period. And even if this transfer of power has a time limit (i.e., until the next elections), it nevertheless requires controls in order that the common will of those who have handed over power remains determinative — for otherwise the will of those who exercise power might become independent from that of the voters. At this point, many would be inclined to call a halt in their reflections and say with satisfaction: if everyone's freedom is guaranteed, the state has reached its goal.

In this way, the freedom of the individual to order his own life is declared to be the real goal of societal life. Community has no value whatever in itself but exists only to allow the individual to be himself. However, if the individual freedom presented here as the highest goal lacks contents, it dissolves into thin air, since individual freedom can exist only when freedoms are correctly ordered. Individual freedom needs measure, for otherwise it turns into violence directed against others. It is not by chance that those who aim at totalitarian rule begin by introducing an anarchic freedom for individuals and a situation in which each one's hand is raised against all the others: by introducing order into this situation, they are enabled to present themselves as the true saviors of mankind. *Thus, freedom requires contents.* We can define it as the safeguarding of human rights, but we can also describe it more broadly as the guarantee that things will go well both with society and with the individual: the one who is ruled, i.e., the one who has handed over power, "can be free, when he recognizes himself, that is to say, his own good, in the common good which the rulers endeavor to bring about."[1]

This reflection has introduced two further concepts alongside the idea of freedom: law and the good. There exists a certain tension between freedom as the existential form of democracy and the contents of freedom (i.e., law and the good),

---

1. H. Kuhn, *Der Staat: Eine philosophische Darstellung* (Munich, 1967), 60.

and contemporary struggles to discover the right form of democracy, and indeed of political life as a whole, are struggles to find the right balance in this tension.

Naturally, we tend to think of freedom as the true good of human beings; all other goods seem controversial today, since we feel that it is all too easy to abuse them. We do not want the state to impose one particular idea of the good on us. The problem becomes even clearer when we employ the concept of truth to clarify the concept of the good, since we think today that respect for the freedom of the individual makes it utterly wrong for the state to decide the question of truth — and this in turn means that we do not think it possible for a community as such to discern truth, and thus truth about what is good. Truth is controversial, and the attempt to impose on all persons what one part of the citizenry holds to be true looks like the enslavement of people's consciences. The concept of "truth" has in fact moved into the zone of antidemocratic intolerance. It is not now a public good, but something private. It may perhaps be the good of specific groups, but it is not the truth of society as a whole. To make this point in other terms: the modern concept of democracy seems indissolubly linked to that of relativism. It is relativism that appears to be the real guarantee of freedom and especially of the very heart of human freedom, namely, freedom of religion and of conscience.

We would all agree on this today. Yet, if we look more closely, we are surely obliged to ask: Must there not be a nonrelativistic kernel in democracy too? For is not democracy ultimately constructed around human rights that are inviolable? Does not democracy appear necessary precisely in order to guarantee and protect these rights? Human rights are not subject to any demand for pluralism and tolerance: on the contrary, they *are* the very substance of tolerance and freedom. Law and freedom can never mean robbing another person of his rights. And this means that a basic element of truth, namely, ethical truth, is indispensable to democracy. We prefer today to speak of values rather than of truth, in order to avoid coming into conflict with the idea of tolerance and with democratic relativism. But such a terminological transposition will not allow us to evade the question I have just posed, since values derive their inviolability precisely from the fact that they are true and that they correspond to true requirements of human existence.

This makes a further question all the more urgent: What is the basis of these values that are valid in the community? Or, to use modern language: What is the basis of those fundamental values that are not subject to the interplay of the majority and the minority in society? How do we recognize them? What is not subject to relativism — and why and how is this the case?

This question is the center of contemporary debates in political philosophy, in our endeavor to achieve a genuine democracy. We could simplify somewhat and say that two basic positions are staked out; these are presented in a number of variants and sometimes even overlap. On the one hand, we find the radical relativistic position which wishes to eliminate the concept of the good (and thereby even more so the concept of that which is true) from politics altogether because it poses a risk to freedom. "Natural law" is rejected because it reeks of metaphysics. And this makes it possible to maintain a consistent relativism: there is ultimately no other principle governing political activity than the decision of the majority, which occupies the position of "truth" in the life of the state. Law can be understood only in purely political terms. In other words, law is whatever the competent organs of the state posit as law. Democracy, therefore, is not defined in terms of its contents, but in a purely functional manner, as a complex of rules that enable the construction of a majority, transfer of power, and change of government. Democracy consists essentially in the mechanisms of election and voting.

This view is opposed by a thesis that affirms that truth is not a product of politics (the majority) but is antecedent to political activity and sheds light on it. It is not praxis that creates truth but truth that makes praxis possible. Political activity is just and promotes freedom when it serves a complex of values and rights that reason makes known to us. The explicit skepticism of relativistic and positivistic theories is countered here by a basic confidence in the ability of human reason to make truth known.[2]

The essential character of these two positions can be seen very clearly in the trial of Jesus, when Pilate asks the Savior: "What is truth?" (John 18:38). One very prominent representative of the strictly relativistic position, the Austrian professor of jurisprudence Hans Kelsen, who later emigrated to America, has published a meditation on this biblical text in which he sets out his view with unmistakable clarity.[3]

We shall return below to Kelsen's political philosophy; let us first see how he expounds the biblical text.

Kelsen sees Pilate's question as an expression of the skepticism that a politician must possess. In this sense, the question is already an answer: truth is unattainable. And we see that this is indeed how Pilate thinks from the fact that he does not even wait for an answer from Jesus but turns immediately to address the crowd. He leaves it to the people to decide the disputed question by means of their vote. Kelsen holds that Pilate acts here as a perfect democrat: since he himself does not know what is just, he leaves it to the majority to decide. In this way, the Austrian scholar portrays Pilate as the emblematic figure of a relativistic and skeptical democracy that is based not on values and truth but on correct procedures. Kelsen seems not to be disturbed by the fact that the outcome of Jesus' trial was the condemnation of an innocent and righteous man. After all,

---

2. This fundamental question in the contemporary debate about the correct understanding of democracy is presented in a very illuminating manner in V. Possenti, *Le società liberali al bivio: Lineamenti di filosofia della società* (Genoa, 1991); see esp. 298ff.

3. For details, see Possenti, *Le società liberali al bivio*, 315–45, and esp. 345f. On the debate with Kelsen, Kuhn, *Der Staat*, 41f., is also helpful.

there is no other truth than that of the majority, and one cannot "get behind" this truth to ask further questions. At one point, Kelsen even goes so far as to say that this relativistic certainty must be imposed, if need be, at the cost of blood and tears. One must be as certain of it as Jesus was certain of his own truth.[4]

The great exegete Heinrich Schlier offered a completely different exposition of this text, one that is much more convincing even from a political point of view. Schlier was writing in the period when National Socialism was preparing to seize power in Germany, and his exposition was a conscious testimony against those groups in the German Protestant churches who were willing to put "faith" and "people" on the same level.[5] Schlier points out that although Jesus in his trial acknowledges the judicial authority of the state represented by Pilate, he also sets limits to this authority by saying that Pilate does not possess this authority on his own account but has it "from above" (19:11). Pilate falsifies his power, and hence also the power of the state, as soon as he ceases to exercise it as the faithful administrator of a higher order that depends on truth and, instead, exploits power to his own advantage. The governor no longer asks what truth is but understands power as sheer, unadulterated power. "As soon as he legitimated his own self, he became the instrument of the judicial murder of Jesus."[6]

What Is the State For?

This demonstrates the questionable nature of a strictly relativistic position. On the other hand, we are all aware today

---

4. See Possenti, *Le società liberali al bivio*, 336.

5. H. Schlier, "Die Beurteilung des Staates im Neuen Testament," first published in 1932 in *Zwischen den Zeiten*; quoted here from his collected essays: H. Schlier, *Die Zeit der Kirche*, 2nd ed. (Freiburg i.Br., 1958), 1–16; see also the essay "Jesus und Pilatus" in the same volume, 56–74.

6. Schlier, *Die Zeit der Kirche*, 3.

of the problems entailed by a position that would make truth fundamental and relevant to democratic praxis. Fear of the Inquisition and the violation of conscience has been too deeply etched in us. Is there any way out of this dilemma? Let us begin by asking what the state in fact is. What is it for, and what is it not for? We will then look at the various answers that are given to these questions and, finally, attempt to arrive at a concluding answer.

What is the state? What purpose does it serve? We could quite simply affirm that it is the task of the state "to regulate human life in society,"[7] creating a balance of freedom and good things that allows each individual to lead a life worthy of man. We could also say that the state guarantees the law, which is a precondition of freedom and of shared prosperity. Governance is an essential element of the state, but this governance is not merely the exercise of power but the safeguard of the rights of each individual and the welfare of all. It is not the task of the state to create mankind's happiness, nor is it the task of the state to create new men. It is not the task of the state to change the world into a paradise — nor can it do so. If it tries, it abandons its own boundaries and posits itself as something absolute. It behaves as if it were God, and, as the Revelation of John shows, this makes it the beast from the abyss, the power of the Antichrist.

In this context, we should always bear two scriptural texts in mind, Romans 13 and Revelation 13, which are only apparently antithetical. The letter to the Romans describes the state in its ordered form, a state that keeps to its own proper boundaries and does not present itself as the source of truth and law. Paul envisages the state as the faithful custodian of good order, enabling people to live well as individuals and as a community. We must obey this state: obedience to the law does not prevent freedom but rather makes freedom possible.

---

7. Ibid., 11.

The Apocalypse paints a different picture: here, the state declares itself to be a god and determines autonomously what is to be counted as righteous and true. Such a state destroys man by denying his true being. It has therefore lost its claim on our obedience.[8]

It is significant that both National Socialism and Marxism basically denied the state and the law. They declared the bond of law to be servitude, claiming to replace it with something higher, the so-called "will of the people" or the "classless society," which was meant to take the place of the state (since the state was the instrument of the hegemony of one single class). In regarding the state and its ordered structures as the foe of the absolute claims made by their own ideology, these demagogues remained at least to some extent aware of what a state really is: the state establishes a relative ordering for life in society, but it cannot answer on its own the question of the meaning of human existence. Not only must it leave space open for something else, perhaps for something higher. It must also receive from outside itself the truth about what is right, since it does not bear this truth in itself. But how and where does this happen? It is time to investigate this question.

The Contradictory Answers to the Questions of the Foundations of Democracy

The Relativistic Theory

As I have said above, two diametrically opposed positions offer answers to these questions, but there are also intermediary views. We have already encountered the first view, that of a strict relativism, in the figure of Hans Kelsen. For him the relationship between religion and democracy is only negative, since one particular characteristic of Christianity is that it

---

8. See ibid., 3–7; 14–16.

teaches absolute truths and values, and this is the exact antithesis of the necessary skepticism of a relativistic democracy. Kelsen understands religion as a heteronomy of the person, whereas democracy retains the autonomy of the person. This also means that the core of democracy is freedom, not the good, for that is something that puts freedom at risk.[9] Today, the American legal philosopher Richard Rorty is the best known representative of this view of democracy. His version of the connection between democracy and relativism expresses to a large extent the average awareness even of Christians today and therefore deserves close attention. Rorty argues that the only criterion for the formulation of law is the widespread conviction held by the majority of the citizens. Democracy does not have access to any other philosophy or any other source of law. Naturally, Rorty is aware that it is ultimately unsatisfactory to appeal to the majority principle as the only source of truth. We see this from his affirmation that pragmatic reason that is orientated to the majority will always include a number of intuitive ideas, such as the rejection of slavery.[10] Here, of course, he is mistaken: for centuries, or even millennia, the sensitivities of the majority did not include this particular intuition, and no one can predict how long the majority will in fact reject slavery. Here we see an empty concept of freedom that can even maintain that the dissolution of the ego, so that it becomes a phenomenon without a center and without an essence, is necessary in order specifically to shape our intuition about the preeminence of freedom. But what if this intuition disappears? What if a majority forms against freedom and tells us that man is not mature enough for freedom but wants and ought to be led?

There is certainly something enticing in the idea that only the majority can make decisions in a democracy and that the

---

9. See Possenti, *Le società liberali al bivio*, 321.
10. Ibid., 293.

only source of law can be those convictions held by citizens who are capable of assembling majority support. For whenever the majority is obliged to accept something that is not willed and decided by this majority, it seems that its freedom is denied and therefore the very essence of democracy is denied. Every other theory appears to assume a dogmatism that undermines self-determination, depriving citizens of the right to make decisions and abolishing their freedom.

On the other hand, one can scarcely deny that the majority is capable of making mistakes. These errors do not concern only peripheral matters. They can call fundamental goods into question so that human dignity and human rights are no longer guaranteed and freedom loses its very raison d'être. It is certainly not always clear to the majority what human rights are or what human dignity really implies. The history of the twentieth century offers dramatic proof that majorities can be seduced and manipulated and that freedom can be destroyed precisely in the name of freedom. We have also seen in our reflections on Kelsen that relativism contains a dogmatism of its own: this position is so sure of itself that it must be imposed even on those who disagree with it. In the last analysis, there is no way of avoiding here the cynicism which is so obvious in Kelsen and Rorty. If the majority, as in the case of Pilate, is always right, then what truly is right must be trampled upon. For then the only thing that counts is the power of the one who is stronger and knows how to win the majority over to his own views.

The Metaphysical and Christian Thesis

There also exists a position that is strictly antithetical to this skeptical relativism. The father of this other view of political activity is Plato, who assumes that only one who himself knows and has experienced the good is capable of ruling well. All sovereignty must be service, i.e., a conscious act whereby one renounces the contemplative height that one has attained and the freedom that this height brings. The act of governing must be a voluntary return into the dark "cave" in which men live. It is only in this way that genuine governance comes about. Anything else is a mere scuffling with illusions in a realm of shadows — and that is in fact what most of political activity is. Plato detects the blindness of average politicians in their fight for power "as if that were a great good."[11] Such reflections bring Plato close to the fundamental biblical idea that truth is not a product of politics. If the relativists genuinely believe this, then they are in fact flirting with totalitarianism even though they seek to establish the primacy of freedom, for they make the majority a kind of divinity against which no further appeal is possible.

Such insights led Jacques Maritain to develop a political philosophy that attempts to draw on the great intuitions of the Bible and make these fruitful for political theory. We need not discuss the historical presuppositions of this philosophy here, although that would certainly be worthwhile. It suffices to note briefly — at the risk of considerable simplification — that in the modern period the concept of democracy developed along two paths and, hence, on differing foundations. In the Anglo-Saxon sphere, democracy was at least partly conceived and realized on the basis of the tradition of natural law and of a fundamental Christian consensus that certainly had a very pragmatic character.[12] In Rousseau, on the other hand, democracy is employed to attack Christian tradition, and he stands at the head of a stream of thought that tends to conceive of democracy as antithetical to Christianity.[13]

Maritain attempted to dissociate the concept of democracy from Rousseau and — as he himself said — free it from the

---

11. *Republic* VII, 520C; see also Possenti, *Le società liberali al bivio*, 290; H. Kuhn, "Plato," in *Klassiker des politischen Denkens*, 3rd ed., ed. H. Maier, H. Rausch, and H. Denzer (Munich, 1969), 1–35.

12. See Kuhn, *Der Staat*, 263ff.

13. See R. Spaemann, *Rousseau: Bürger ohne Vaterland* (Munich, 1980).

Freemasons' dogmas of necessary progress, anthropological optimism, deification of the individual, and forgetfulness of the human person.[14] For him, the primary right of a people to govern itself can never become a right to decide everything. "Government of the people" and "government for the people" belong together, and an equilibrium must be reached between the will of the people and the values that supply the goal of political action. In this sense, Maritain developed a three-fold personalism, ontological, axiological, and social, which we cannot discuss in detail here.[15]

It is clear that Christianity is considered here as the source of knowledge, antecedent to the political action on which it sheds light. In order to exclude any suspicion that Christianity might desire a political absolutism. V. Possenti writes, in keeping with Maritain, that the source of truth for politics is not Christianity as revealed religion but Christianity as leaven and a form of life which has proved its worth in the course of history. The truth about the good supplied by the Christian tradition becomes an insight of human reason and hence a rational principle. This truth does not inflict violence on reason or on politics by means of some kind of dogmatism.[16] Naturally, this presupposes a certain amount of optimism about the evidential character of morality and of Christianity, and the relativists would not accept this. This brings us back to the critical point of democratic theory and of its Christian exposition.

Evidential Character of Morality? *Mediating Positions*

Before we attempt to give an answer, it is helpful to look first at the mediating positions that do not completely fall into one of the two camps. Possenti mentions N. Bobbio, K. Popper, and J. Schumpeter as representatives of such a middle way; the

---

14. Possenti, *Le società liberali al bivio*, 309.
15. See ibid., 308–10.
16. Ibid., 308ff.

Cartesian P. Bayle (1647–1706) may be considered an early forerunner of this position since his starting point is a strict distinction between metaphysical and moral truth. In Bayle's view, political life does not require metaphysics. Metaphysical questions may safely remain controversial; they are assigned to a pluralist sphere that is not touched by politics. Practical truth is a sufficient basis for the existence of the community of a state. Bayle is optimistic about the possibility of discerning this practical truth. Subsequent generations lost this optimism long ago, but he could still hold that moral truth is obvious to everyone. There is only one single, universal, and necessary morality, a true and clear light perceived by all persons, provided only that they open their eyes. This one moral truth comes from God, and every individual law and norm must take this truth as its point of reference.[17] Bayle is simply describing here the universal consciousness of his own century. The basic moral insights revealed by Christianity were so obvious to all and so incontrovertible that even in the conflict between confessions they could be regarded as insights that every rational man took for granted. They possessed a rational evidential quality that remained unaffected by the dogmatic disputes of a divided Christendom.

But what seemed a compelling, God-given insight of reason retained its evidential character only for as long as the entire culture, the entire existential context, bore the imprint of Christian tradition. The moral dimension lost its evidential quality with the crumbling of the fundamental Christian consensus. All that remained was a naked reason that refused to learn from any historical reality but was willing to listen only to its own self. Reason, by cutting off its roots in the faith of a historical and religious culture and wishing now to be nothing more than empirical reason, became blind. Where that which is experimentally verifiable became the only accepted shared

---

17. See ibid., 291.

certainty, the only criterion left to evaluate those truths that went beyond the purely material sphere was their functioning, the interplay between majority and minority. As we have seen, however, this isolation necessarily leads to cynicism and to the destruction of man. The real problem that confronts us today is reason's blindness to the entire nonmaterial dimension of reality.

It will suffice here to look briefly at the social philosophy of K. Popper, who attempts to hang onto Bayle's fundamental vision and salvage it for a relativistic age. Popper's vision of an open society includes free discussion and institutions that guard freedom and protect the disadvantaged. The values on which democracy — as the best form of realizing the open society — is based are recognized by means of a moral faith. They are not to be justified by an appeal to reason. A process of criticism and insight akin to the advancement of science brings us closer to truth. This means that the principles of society cannot be justified or discussed. In the end, one must make a decision about them.[18]

Clearly, many elements contribute to this vision. On the one hand, Popper sees that in the process of free discussion a moral truth possesses no evidential quality. On the other hand, however, he holds that it is possible to grasp this evidential quality in a kind of rational faith. Popper knows perfectly well that the majority principle cannot be permitted to hold sway unconditionally. Bayle's great idea of the shared certainty of reason on moral issues has shrunk here to a faith that feels its way forward through discussions — and yet, even though the ground on which it stands is shaky, this faith discloses fundamental elements of moral truth and removes them from the realm of pure functionalism. If we look at the whole picture, we may surely say that this slender remnant of rational basic moral certainty

---

18. Ibid., 301.

is not the product of reason alone but is based on a surviving remnant of insights from the Jewish-Christian tradition. Even this remnant has itself long ceased to be an undisputed certainty. But a minimum of morality is somehow still accessible in the decomposing Christian culture.

Let us look back before we attempt our own answer. We must reject the absolute state that posits itself as the source of truth and law. We must also reject a strict relativism and functionalism, because the elevation of truth to the unique source of law threatens the moral dignity of man and tends toward totalitarianism. This means that the spectrum of acceptable theories would go from Maritain to Popper. Maritain has the greatest confidence in the rational evidential quality of the moral truth of Christianity and of the Christian image of man. Popper exemplifies the least measure of confidence, but this minimum is just enough to ward off a collapse into positivism.

I do not wish to offer a new theory about the relationship between the state and moral truth, either complementing these authors or mediating between them. All I wish is to attempt to summarize the insights that we have encountered so far. They could form a kind of platform that permits a conversation between those political philosophies that in some way or other consider Christianity and its moral message to be a point of reference of political conduct, without thereby blurring the borders between politics and faith.

SUMMARY AND CONCLUSIONS

I believe that we can summarize the conclusions of our examination of the modern debate in the following seven statements:

1. The state is not itself the source of truth and morality. It cannot produce truth from its own self by means of an

ideology based on people or race or class or some other
entity. Nor can it produce truth via the majority. The state
is not absolute.

2. The goal of the state cannot consist in a freedom without defined contents. In order to establish a meaningful
   and viable ordering of life in society, the state requires a
   minimum of truth, of knowledge of the good, that cannot
   be manipulated. Otherwise, as Augustine says, it will sink
   to the level of a smoothly functioning band of robbers,
   because, like such a band, its definition would be purely
   functional. It would not be defined on the basis of that
   justice which is good for everyone.

3. Accordingly, the state must receive from outside itself the
   essential measure of knowledge and truth with regard to
   that which is good.

4. This "outside" might, in the best possible scenario, be
   the pure insight of reason. It would be the task of an independent philosophy to cultivate this insight and keep
   watch over it. In practice, however, such a pure rational
   evidential quality independent of history does not exist.
   Metaphysical and moral reason comes into action only in
   a historical context. At one and the same time, it depends
   on this context and transcends it. In fact, all states have
   recognized and applied moral reason on the basis of antecedent religious traditions, which also provided moral
   education. Naturally, openness to reason and the measure
   of knowledge of the good differs greatly in the historical
   religions, just as the relationship between state and religion
   has taken different forms. We find throughout history the
   temptation to identify the state with divinity and to ab-
   solutize it in religious terms. But we certainly also find
   positive models of a relationship between moral knowledge based on religion and the good ordering of the state.

Indeed, one may say that the great institutions of religion and the state display a fundamental consensus about important elements of what is morally good and that this consensus points to a shared rationality.

5. Christian faith has proved to be the most universal and rational religious culture. Even today, it offers reason the basic structure of moral insight which, if it does not actually lead to some kind of evidential quality, at least furnishes the basis of a rational moral faith without which no society can endure.

6. Accordingly, as I have already observed, the state receives its basic support from outside: not from a mere reason that is inadequate in the moral realm, but from a reason that has come to maturity in the historical form of faith. This distinction must not be canceled out: the Church may not exalt itself to become a state, nor may it seek to work as an organ of power in the state or beyond the state boundaries, for then it would make itself precisely that absolute state that it is meant to rule out. By merging with the state, the Church would destroy both the essence of the state and its own essence.

7. The Church remains something "outside" the state, for only thus can both Church and state be what they are meant to be. Like the state, the Church too must remain in its own proper place and within its boundaries. It must respect its own being and its own freedom, precisely in order to be able to perform for the state the service that the latter requires. The Church must exert itself with all its vigor so that in it there may shine forth the moral truth that it offers to the state and that ought to become evident to the citizens of the state. This truth must be vigorous within the Church, and it must form men, for only then it

will have the power to convince others and to be a force working like a leaven for all of society.[19]

Closing Reflection: Heaven and Earth

This gives a new importance to a Christian doctrine of which little was heard in the twentieth century. It is expressed in Paul's words: "Our commonwealth is in heaven" (Phil. 3:20).[20] The New Testament affirms this conviction with great emphasis. It understands the city in heaven not merely as an ideal reality, but as a completely real affair. The new homeland toward which we are journeying is the interior criterion that governs our life and the hope that sustains us in the present day. The New Testament writers know that this city already exists and that we already belong to it, even if we are still en route. The letter to the Hebrews expresses this idea with particular urgency: "Here we have no lasting city, but we seek the city which is to come" (13:14). The author writes about the presence of this city, which is an effective reality even now: "You have come to Mount Zion and to the city of the living God, the heavenly Jerusalem" (12:22). Accordingly, we may say of Christians what was once said of the patriarchs of Israel: they are foreigners and resident aliens, since their whole efforts tend toward their future fatherland (11:13–16).

For a long time now, Christians have tended to avoid quoting these texts, since they appear to alienate man from the earth and prevent him from fulfilling his innerworldly task, which is also a political task. Nietzsche called out, over a hundred years ago: "Brothers, remain faithful to the earth!" And

---

19. Soloviev's reflections on Church and state, which deserve to be pondered anew, go in the same direction, although the idea of "theocracy" is not tenable in the form in which he elaborated it. See *La grande controverse et la politique chrétienne* (Paris, 1953), 129–68.

20. On what follows, see Schlier, *Die Zeit der Kirche*, 7ff.

the mighty Marxist tendency that was hammered into us held that time devoted to heaven is time wasted. Bertold Brecht said we should leave heaven to the sparrows,[21] while we ourselves take care of the earth and make it a place where we can live.

In reality, it is precisely this "eschatological" attitude that guarantees the state its own rights while simultaneously resisting absolutism by indicating the boundaries both of the state and of the Church in the world. Where this fundamental attitude prevails, the Church knows that it cannot be a state here on earth, for it is aware that the definitive state lies elsewhere, and that it cannot set up the City of God on earth. It respects the earthly state as an institution belonging to historical time, with rights and laws that the Church recognizes. This is why it demands loyalty and collaboration with the earthly state, even when this is not a Christian state (Rom. 13:1; 1 Pet. 2:13–17; 1 Tim. 2:2). By both demanding loyal cooperation with the state and respect for its specific nature and its limitations, the Church provides an education in those virtues that allow a state to become good. At the same time, it puts up a barrier against the omnipotence of the state. Because one "must obey God rather than men" (Acts 5:29), and because the Church has learned from the Word of God what is good and what is evil, it sounds the cry for resistance wherever the state might demand something genuinely evil and opposed to God.

The fact that Christians are journeying toward the other city does not alienate them. In reality, it is this that allows us to be healthy and our states to be healthy. For if men have nothing more to expect than what this world offers them, and if they may and must demand all this from the state, they destroy both their own selves and every human society. If we do not want to get entangled anew in the tentacles of totalitarianism, we must look beyond the state, which is only one part, not the totality.

---

21. [Translator's note:] There is a play on words in German: *Himmel* means both "heaven" and "sky."

There is no antithesis between hope for heaven and loyalty to the earth, since this hope is also hope for the earth. While we hope for something greater and definitive, we Christians may and must bring hope into that which is transitory, into the world of our states.

PART
II

RESPONSIBILITY
FOR PEACE

Orientations

☙

5

If You Want Peace...

Conscience and Truth

❧

Today, especially within Catholic moral theology, conscience has become the core issue with regard to morality and our discovery of what constitutes moral conduct. This debate centers on the concepts of freedom and norm, autonomy and heteronomy, self-determination and determination by an external authority. Conscience is presented here as the bulwark of freedom against those who seek to narrow our lives through the use of authority. Two antithetical conceptions of Catholicism are proposed. On the one hand, we find a renewed understanding of the essence of Catholicism that understands Christian faith on the basis of freedom and sees this faith as a principle that sets people free. On the other hand, we find a superseded "preconciliar" model that subjects Christian existence to an authority that issues norms to regulate people's lives even in the most intimate spheres and attempts in this way to maintain its power over them. It seems therefore that we have a conflict between two antithetical models, *morality of conscience* and *morality of authority*. The freedom of the Christian is safeguarded by the primal proposition of the moral tradition, that the *conscience is the highest norm* and that one must follow it even against authority. When authority — in this case the

Church's magisterium — speaks on matters of morality, it supplies material that helps the conscience form its own judgment,
but ultimately it is only conscience that has the last word. Some
authors express this ultimately decisive authority of conscience
by saying that conscience is infallible.[1]

At this point, we may surely make an objection. It is indisputable that *one must always follow a clear verdict of
conscience,* or at least that one may not act against such a verdict. But it is quite a different matter to assume that the verdict
of conscience (or what one takes to be such a verdict) is always
correct, i.e., infallible — for if that were so, it would mean that
there is no truth, at least in matters of morality and religion,
which are the foundations of our very existence. Since verdicts
of conscience contradict one another, there would exist only a
truth of the subject, which would be reduced to the truthful-
ness of that subject. No door or window would lead out of the
individual subject into the totality or into that which is shared
with other subjects. If we think this through, we realize that

---

1. It appears that J. G. Fichte was the first to propose this thesis: "The
conscience never errs and can never err," since it is "itself the judge of all convictions" and "knows no higher judge above itself. It bears the responsibility
for the final decision, and there is no appeal against conscience" (*System der
Sittenlehre,* 1798, III, §15; *Werke* (Berlin, 1971), 4:174). See H. Reiner, "Gewissen," in *Historisches Wörterbuch der Philosophie,* ed. J. Ritter, 3:574–92; here,
586. Kant had already formulated the arguments against this proposition, and
Hegel stated them even more profoundly: he regarded conscience "as a formal subjectivity...continuously on the point of changing into evil": see Reiner,
"Gewissen." Nevertheless, we are witnessing a revival of this thesis in popular
theological literature today. I find a mediatory position in E. Schockenhoff, *Das
umstrittene Gewissen* (Mainz, 1990). He reckons explicitly with the possibility
that conscience may fail to do its proper job "because it loses its faith in the other
demand of the moral law, the mutual acknowledgment of free rational beings"
(139), but appeals to arguments by Linsenmann when he rejects the concept of the
"erring conscience": "With regard to the quality of the conscience as such, it is
meaningless to speak of error, since there is no superior platform from which one
could identify such an error" (136). But why not? Is there not a truth about the
good to which we all have access? It is indeed true that Schockenhoff himself goes
on to qualify considerably the sentence I have quoted from p. 136. But this only
leaves me even more puzzled by his assertion that the concept of an erring conscience is untenable. M. Honecker, *Einführung in die theologische Ethik* (Berlin,
1990), 138ff., has helpful remarks on this question.

this would also mean that there is no genuine freedom and that the supposed verdicts of conscience were mere reflexes to antecedent social circumstances.

This reflection surely shows that the proposed antithesis between freedom and authority leaves out something important and that there must be something deeper than this if freedom and human existence itself are to have a meaning.

A Conversation about the Erring Conscience and Some Initial Conclusions

This shows that the question about conscience leads us to the core of the moral problem and, hence, to the question of human existence itself. I do not wish to present this question here in the form of a strictly conceptual reflection, since that would necessarily move on a very abstract plane. Rather, I should like to take a "narrative" path, beginning with the story of my own interest in this problem. I first became aware of it in all its urgency at the beginning of my academic career. An older colleague, who was deeply moved by the difficulties involved in being a Christian in our time, stated in a debate that we ought really to be grateful to God that he had given so many people the gift of being unbelievers with a good conscience. For if their eyes were opened and they became believers, they would not be able to endure the burden of faith and its moral obligations in this world of ours. As things were, since they were traveling in good conscience along another path, they could nevertheless attain salvation.

What shocked me in this assertion was not so much the idea of an erring conscience bestowed by God himself, a cunning device that allowed him to save men — as if he saved them precisely by blinding their eyes. No, I was disturbed by the idea that faith was a virtually intolerable burden, something only the really strong could shoulder. Perhaps it would be going too far to call faith a punishment, but it certainly posed extremely high demands that were difficult to satisfy. In other words, faith made salvation harder, not easier. One should therefore rejoice if the obligation to believe is not imposed upon one, since that would mean being bowed down by the yoke of the morality of the Catholic Church. An erring conscience, which makes life easier and points to a more human path in life, would be a genuine grace, and even the normal way to find salvation. Untruth, remaining far away from truth, would be better for man than truth. Truth would not be something that sets us free, but something from which we need to be set free. Man would be more at home in the darkness than in the light. Faith would not be a good gift of the good God, but a terrible fate. But if that is correct, how would it be possible to rejoice in the faith? What could give us the courage to hand this faith on to others? Would it not actually be better to spare them the burden of believing or actively to prevent them from coming to the faith? It is obvious that ideas of this kind have paralyzed the willingness on the part of Christians in recent decades to engage in evangelization, and this is logical: one who experiences faith as a heavy load, as an exacting moral challenge, will not want to invite others to believe. One will prefer to leave them in the supposed freedom of their good conscience.

The man who spoke in these terms was an honest believer, and I would even call him a strictly observant Catholic, a man who fulfilled his religious obligations with conviction and exactitude. But the kind of experience of the faith that he expressed can only unsettle others. If such an idea of faith were to spread, it would have fatal consequences. I am convinced that the *traumatic aversion* that many people feel *toward* what they regard as *"preconciliar"* Catholicism has its roots in their *encounter with* this kind of *faith*, which was *nothing more than a burden*.

This poses very fundamental questions. Can such a faith in fact be an encounter with truth? Is the truth about the human person and God so sad and so difficult, or does truth not lie precisely in overcoming such legalism? Does it not lie in freedom? But, then, where does freedom lead? What path does it show us? At the end of this essay, we must return to these fundamental problems of Christian existence today. But first we must look at the core of our subject, the question of conscience.

As I have said, I was initially shocked by the caricature of faith that I thought I saw in my colleague's argument. Further reflection suggested that he was employing a false concept of conscience. His argument was that an erring conscience saves man by protecting him from the terrifying demands made by truth. Conscience was not envisaged here as a window that makes it possible for man to see the truth that is common to us all, the truth that is our basis and sustains us. My colleague did not understand conscience as making possible a shared knowledge that could generate a shared will and a shared responsibility. Here, conscience was not the decision made by man in favor of the foundations that supported his existence; it was not the power to perceive the highest and most essential of all realities. On the contrary, here conscience was a cloak thrown over human subjectivity, allowing man to elude the clutches of reality and to hide from it. This meant that the speaker presupposed the idea of conscience found in liberalism. Conscience does not reveal the road of truth, which we can take and so be saved — for either truth does not exist at all, or else it is impossible for us to meet its demands. And this makes "conscience" the justification of a human subjectivity that refuses to let itself be called into question, as well as of social conformism that is meant to function as an average value between the various subjectivities and thereby enable human beings to live together. There is no longer any need to feel obliged to look for truth, nor may one doubt the average attitude and customary praxis. It suffices to be convinced of one's own correctness and to conform to others. Man is reduced to his superficial conviction, and the less depth he possesses, the better off he is.

In the course of that particular conversation, these reflections occurred to me only in passing. Shortly afterward, however, in a debate we held about the justifying force of an erring conscience, they emerged with pitiless clarity. One colleague suggested the thesis that, if it were generally true that an erring conscience could lead to salvation, then even the SS troops under Hitler would have been justified and would now be in heaven, since they had committed their evil deeds out of fanatical conviction and without the least disturbance to their consciences. Another colleague responded, as if he were stating the most obvious thing in the world: "Yes, that is so!" He argued that there was not the slightest doubt that Hitler and his collaborators were deeply convinced of their cause and could not in fact have acted differently. Therefore, despite all the objective horror of their deeds, they had acted morally, from a subjective perspective. And since they were following their conscience, even though it was misdirected, their conduct must be acknowledged as moral. There is thus no doubt that they attained eternal salvation.

Since that second conversation, I have been absolutely certain that there is something wrong with the theory of the justifying force of the subjective conscience. In other words, a concept of conscience that leads to such inferences is false. A firm subjective conviction, with the consequent lack of doubts and scruples, does not justify anyone.

About thirty years later, I read an essay by the psychologist Albert Görres that summarized briefly the insights that I had slowly tried to formulate for myself and that I wish to set out here. Görres points out that guilt feelings, or the ability to recognize one's guilt, is an essential element of man's psychological makeup. The guilt feeling that shatters a conscience's false calm and the criticism made by my conscience of my self-satisfied existence are signals that we need just as much as we need the physical pain that lets us know that our normal vital functions have been disturbed. One who is no longer capable of seeing his own guilt is psychologically ill, "a living corpse, a theatrical mask," as Görres puts it.[2] "Inhuman persons, monsters — it is people like these who have no guilt feelings. Hitler may have had none; nor may Himmler or Stalin. Mafia bosses may have none, but it is more likely that they have merely suppressed their awareness of the skeletons in their closets. And the aborted guilt feelings. . . . Everyone needs guilt feelings. . . . Everyone needs guilt feelings."[3]

There is in fact a scriptural text that could have prevented the diagnoses put forward by my colleagues and shown them that the theory of justification by means of an erring conscience is untenable. Psalm 19:12 contains words that deserve constant meditation: "But who can discern his errors? Clear thou me from hidden faults." The wisdom of the Old Testament takes a very different line from my professorial colleagues: the *loss of the ability to see* one's guilt, the *falling silent of conscience* in so many areas, is a *more dangerous illness of the soul than* guilt that is *recognized* as *guilt*. One who no longer pays heed to the fact that killing is a sin has fallen more deeply than one who still recognizes the abhorrent quality of his actions, since the former person is further away from truth and from repentance. It is not by chance that the self-righteous person is revealed in the encounter with Jesus to be the one who is really lost: when the tax collector with all his undisputed sins is more righteous in the eyes of God than the Pharisee with all his genuinely good deeds (Luke 18:9–14), this is not because the sins of the tax collector were not sins or the good deeds of the Pharisee not good deeds. Jesus does not intend to say that man's good deeds are not good in God's sight or that his evil deeds are not evil (or, at any rate, not all that serious).

---

2. A. Görres, "Schuld und Schuldgefühle," *Internationale katholische Zeitschrift "Communio"* 13 (1984): 434.

3. Ibid., 442.

The reason for this paradoxical verdict by God is directly connected to the question we are examining here. The Pharisee is no longer aware that he too is guilty. He is perfectly at ease with his own conscience. But this silence of his conscience makes it impossible for God and men to penetrate his carapace — whereas the cry of conscience that torments the tax collector opens him to receive truth and love. Jesus can work effectively among sinners because they have not become inaccessible behind the screen of an erring conscience, which would put them out of reach of the changes that God awaits from them — and from us. Jesus cannot work effectively among the righteous because they sense no need for forgiveness and repentance; their conscience no longer accuses them but only justifies them.

We find the same idea in different terms in Paul, who tells us that the *Gentiles knew without the law what God expected* of them (Rom. 2:1–16). This passage deals a death-blow to the *entire theory of salvation through ignorance.* Truth is present in man in a manner that cannot be rejected: and this is the same truth of the Creator that also took written form in the revelation of salvation history. Man can *see the truth of God* in the foundations of his created being. *To fail to see this is guilt.* If we refuse to see the truth, this "no" of the will that prevents knowledge is guilt. The warning lamp fails to light up because we deliberately avert our eyes from something we do not want to see.[4]

At this point in our reflections, we can draw our first conclusions to help answer the question about the essence of conscience. We can now say that *it is impossible to identify* man's *conscience with* the *self-awareness* of the ego, *with* his *subjective certainty* about himself and his moral conduct. This consciousness may be a mere reflex of the social environment and of the opinions widespread there. It may also

---

4. See Honecker, *Einführung in die theologische Ethik*, 130.

indicate a lack of self-criticism, a failure to listen to the depths of one's own soul. In the aftermath of the collapse of the Marxist systems in Eastern Europe, the situation that came to light confirms this diagnosis. The most alert and honest spirits among the newly liberated peoples speak of a terrible neglect of the soul that arose in the years of false education. They speak of a blunting of the moral sensitivity, which represents a more terrible loss and danger than the economic damage that occurred.

At the beginning of his time in office, in the summer of 1990, the patriarch of Moscow emphasized this in impressive words. He lamented that those who lived in a system of deceit had lost much of their powers of perception. Society had lost the ability to feel compassion, and human emotions had withered away. An entire generation had become impervious to the good and was incapable of humane deeds. "We must bring society back to the eternal moral values," he said. In other words, the capacity to hear God's voice in the heart of man, a capacity that is almost extinguished, must be developed anew. *It is only in an initial phase that* error, *the erring conscience, is comfortable.* When conscience falls silent and we do nothing to resist it, the consequence is the dehumanization of the world and a deadly danger.

To put this in other terms, the identification of conscience with the superficial consciousness and the reduction of man to his subjectivity do not liberate but rather enslave. They do this by making us completely dependent on prevailing opinions, indeed lowering the level of these opinions day by day. To identify conscience with a superficial state of conviction is to equate it with a certainty that merely seems rational, a certainty woven from self-righteousness, conformism, and intellectual laziness. Conscience is degraded to a mechanism that produces excuses for one's conduct, although in reality conscience is meant to make the subject transparent to the divine, thereby revealing man's authentic dignity and greatness. At the same time, *the reduction of conscience to a subjective certainty* means the *removal of truth*.

Psalm 19 anticipates Jesus' understanding of sin and right-eousness and asks to be set free from the guilt of which the one who prays is unaware. It thus indicates what we have just said: certainly, one must follow the erring conscience. But the *removal of truth,* which *took place earlier* and now takes its revenge in the form of an erring conscience, *is the real guilt* that lulls man in false security and ultimately abandons him to solitude in a pathless wasteland.

NEWMAN AND SOCRATES — SIGNPOSTS TO CONSCIENCE

Let us pause for a moment here, before we attempt to for-mulate comprehensive answers to the question about what conscience truly is. We must first extend somewhat the basis of our considerations, going beyond the personal sphere that was our starting point. Naturally, it is not my intention to offer a learned treatise about the history of the various theo-ries of conscience; this has in fact been examined in a number of recent works.[5] I should like to take only a few examples, remaining in the narrative mode, so to speak. We begin with the figure of Cardinal John Henry Newman, whose entire life and work could be called one great commentary on the ques-tion of conscience. Here too, I shall not present Newman in the categories of professional theology. Space does not allow me to consider individual details in his concept of conscience. All I wish to do is indicate the place of this concept in the

---

5. Apart from the important article by H. Reiner and the book by Schocken-hoff mentioned above, see A. Laun, *Das Gewissen: Oberste Norm sittlichen Handelns* (Innsbruck, 1984); idem, *Aktuelle Probleme der Moraltheologie* (Vienna, 1991), 31–64; J. Gründel, ed. *Das Gewissen: Subjektive Willkür oder oberste Norm?* (Düsseldorf, 1990); for a synthesis and overview, see K. Golser, "Gewissen," in *Neues Lexikon der christlichen Moral,* ed. H. Rotter and G. Virt (Innsbruck and Vienna, 1990), 278–86.

totality of Newman's life and thought. The insights that we gain here will open our eyes to the problems of the present day and reveal the link to history, i.e., to the great witnesses to conscience and to the origin of the Christian doctrine of a life lived in accordance with conscience.

To speak of Newman and conscience is to evoke the famous words in his letter to the duke of Norfolk (1874): "Certainly, if I am obliged to bring religion into after-dinner toasts (which indeed does not seem quite the thing), I shall drink — to the Pope, if you please, — still, to Conscience first, and to the Pope afterwards."[6] Newman intended this to be a clear confession of his faith in the papacy, in response to the objections raised by Gladstone to the dogma of infallibility. At the same time, against erroneous forms of ultramontanism, he meant it to be an interpretation of the papacy, which can be understood correctly only when it is seen in connection with the primacy of conscience — not in opposition to this primacy, but based on it and guaranteeing it. It is difficult for people today to grasp this point, since they think on the basis of an antithesis between authority and subjectivity. Conscience is seen as standing on the side of subjectivity and as an expression of the freedom of the subject, while authority is regarded as the limitation of this freedom, or indeed a threat to it, if not its actual negation. We must look somewhat more deeply here if we are to learn once again how to understand a vision in which this kind of antithesis has no validity.

The intermediate concept that holds these two together for Newman is truth. I would not hesitate to say that truth is the central idea in Newman's intellectual striving. Conscience is central to his thinking because truth is the heart of everything.

6. *Certain Difficulties Felt by Anglicans in Catholic Teaching Considered* (London, 1900), 2:261; see J. Honoré, *Newman, Sa vie et sa pensée* (Paris, 1988), 65; I. Ker, *John Henry Newman: A Biography* (Oxford, 1990), 688ff.; on his doctrine of conscience, see J. Arzt, *Newman-Lexikon* (Mainz, 1975), 396–400. See also A. Läpple, *Der Einzelne in der Kirche: Wesenszüge einer Theologie des Einzelnen nach J. H. Newman* (Munich, 1952).

In other words, the centrality of the concept of conscience in Newman is linked to the antecedent centrality of the concept of truth; only this latter concept allows us to understand what Newman means by "conscience." The dominance of the idea of conscience in Newman does not mean that this nineteenth-century theologian maintains a philosophy or theology of subjectivity in opposition to "objective" neo-scholasticism. It is indeed correct to say that the subject receives a quality of attention in Newman that had been unknown in Catholic theology since Augustine. But his attention echoes that of Augustine, not that of the subjectivist philosophy of the modern period.

When he was created cardinal, Newman avowed that his entire life had been a struggle against liberalism. We might add: also against the kind of Christian subjectivism that he encountered in the evangelical movement of his age, although this had permitted him to take the first steps along his lifelong path of conversion.[7] For Newman, conscience does not mean that it is the subject that has the final word vis-à-vis the claims made by authority in a world devoid of truth, a world that lives on the basis of a compromise between the claims made by the subject and the claims of societal order. Rather, conscience signifies the perceptible and commanding presence of the voice of truth in the subject itself. Conscience means the abolition of mere subjectivity when man's intimate sphere is touched by the truth that comes from God. The verse that Newman wrote in Sicily in 1833 is significant: "I loved to choose and see my path; but now / Lead thou me on."[8] Newman's conversion to Catholicism was not a matter of his own personal taste or of a subjective need of his soul. As late as 1844, on the threshold

---

7. See C. S. Dessain, *John Henry Newman* (London, 1966); G. Biemer, *J. H. Newman, Leben und Werk* (Mainz, 1989).

8. From the well-known poem "Lead, Kindly Light"; see I. Ker, *John Henry Newman: A Biography*, 79; C. S. Dessain, *John Henry Newman* (Freiburg, 1981), 98f.

of his conversion, he wrote that no one could take a more unfavorable view than he himself of the contemporary state of Roman Catholicism.[9] He was convinced that he must obey the truth that he had recognized, rather than his own taste, even at the price of his own feelings and of the ties of friendship formed with those who until then had been his companions. It seems to me characteristic that Newman, when listing the virtues, places truth above goodness — or, to make this point in language with which we are more familiar today, above consensus, above what is acceptable within the group.

I believe that when we speak of "a man of conscience" we are referring to these attitudes. A man of conscience is one who never purchases comfort, well-being, success, public prestige, or approval by prevalent opinion if the price is the renunciation of truth. Here, Newman agrees with that other great British witness to conscience St. Thomas More, who did not in the least regard conscience as the expression of his subjective tenacity or of an eccentric heroism. He saw himself as one of those timorous martyrs who reach the point of obeying their conscience only after hesitation and much questioning, and this is an act of obedience to that truth which must rank higher than every social authority and every kind of personal taste.[10] This indicates two criteria for a genuine word spoken by the conscience: it is not identical with one's own wishes and taste; nor is it identical with that which is more advantageous, socially speaking, with the consensus of a group or with the claims made by political or societal power.

Let us look briefly at the problems that vex our own age. The individual may not purchase his rise in society and his well-being at the price of betrayal of the truth that he has come to recognize; nor may humanity as a whole do so. It

---

9. *Correspondence of J. H. Newman with J. Keble and Others* (London, 1917), 351, 364; see Dessain, *John Henry Newman* (Freiburg, 1981), 163.

10. See P. Berglar, *Die Stunde des Thomas Morus*, 3rd ed. (Olten and Freiburg, 1981), 155ff.

is here that we touch on the neuralgic point of the modern age: the concept of truth has in practice been abandoned and replaced by the concept of progress. Progress itself "is" truth. But this apparent elevation deprives progress of all contents; it dissolves into nothing. For if there is no direction, everything can be interpreted either as progress or as regress.

Einstein's theory of relativity refers as such to the physical cosmos, but it seems to me that it also offers an apt description of the situation of the intellectual cosmos of our time. This theory postulates that there exist no fixed systems of reference within the universe. It is our act of definition, when we declare one particular system to be a point of reference, that allows us to attempt to measure the totality. We are in fact obliged to do so, for there is no other way in which we can arrive at conclusions, but it would always be possible to define things differently. This affirmation about the physical cosmos mirrors the second Copernican revolution in our fundamental relation to reality. We have lost sight of truth as such, the absolute, the basic point of reference of our thought, and this is why — intellectually speaking, not only physically — there is no longer any "up" or "down." There are no directions in a world that lacks fixed points for measuring. What we take to be a direction is not based on a criterion that is itself true but only on our decision, and that means, in the final analysis, on utilitarian considerations. In this kind of "relativistic" context, teleological or consequentialist ethics becomes ultimately nihilistic, even if it is unaware of this. And if we look more closely, we will see that talk about "conscience" in such a world view is merely a way of saying that there is no genuine conscience in the sense of a *con-scientia*, a "knowing with" truth. Each one decides on his own criteria. In this universal relativity, no one can help anyone else in this matter, still less lay down rules for another person to follow.

This shows us how radical the modern debate about ethics and about the center of ethics, the conscience, really is. I believe that the only parallel to this in the history of ideas is the dispute between Socrates/Plato and the Sophists, which explores the primal decision to be made between two basic attitudes, namely, the confidence that man is capable of perceiving truth and a world view in which it is only man himself who posits the criteria he will follow.[11]

I am convinced that it is this primal question that explains how Socrates, a pagan, could in a certain sense become the prophet of Jesus Christ. The way of doing philosophy that was inspired by Socrates took up this question and thus received what we might call a "salvation-historical privilege," which made it a suitable vessel for the Christian Logos, which is concerned with liberation by means of truth and liberation for truth. If we detach Socrates' controversy from the contingent elements of its historical framework, we soon see that this is essentially the same controversy that rages today (with other arguments and other names). If we give up belief in the capacity of man to perceive truth, this leads initially to a purely formalistic use of words and concepts. In turn, the elimination of substance from our words and concepts leads to a pure formalism of judgment, in the past as in the present. One no longer asks *what* a man actually thinks. The verdict on his thinking is readily available, if one succeeds in cataloguing it under an appropriate formal category — conservative, reactionary, fundamentalist, progressive, revolutionary. The assignment to a formal schema is enough to dispense one from actually looking at the contents of what is being said. The same tendency can be seen even more strongly in art. It is irrelevant *what* it depicts; it may be a glorification of God or

---

11. On the debate between Socrates and the Sophists, see J. Pieper, "Missbrauch der Sprache — Missbrauch der Macht," in idem, *Über die Schwierigkeit zu glauben* (Munich, 1974), 255–82; idem, *Kümmert euch nicht um Sokrates* (Munich, 1966). Romano Guardini, *Der Tod des Sokrates*, 5th ed. (Mainz and Paderborn, 1987), emphatically urges that the question of truth is the core of all Socrates' philosophical endeavors.

of the devil. The only criterion is the formal skill employed by the artist.

And this brings us to the heart of the matter. Where contents no longer count, where a pure praxeology takes over, skill becomes the highest criterion. This, however, means that power becomes the category that dominates everything, whether in a revolutionary or a reactionary sense. And that is precisely the perverse form of similarity to God of which we read in the story of the fall of Adam and Eve: the path of mere skill, the path of pure power, is the imitation of an idol, not the enactment of our similarity to God. Man as man is characterized by the fact that he asks not what he can do but what he ought to do, and that he is open to the voice of truth and to the claim it makes upon him. I believe that Socrates' philosophical endeavors are ultimately concerned with this point. Indeed, this is the core of the testimony of all the martyrs. They pay with their lives for their conviction that man is capable of perceiving truth and that this ability both sets a limit to all power and guarantees his resemblance to God. It is precisely in this way that the martyrs are the great witnesses to conscience, to the capacity bestowed on man to go beyond the question of what he can do and to perceive what he ought to do. For it is this that makes possible genuine progress and genuine ascent.

Systematic Consequences: The Two Levels of Conscience

Anamnesis

After these excursions through the history of ideas, it is now time to present conclusions, to formulate a concept of conscience. I agree with the *medieval tradition* that there are *two levels in this concept* that must be clearly *distinguished* from each other but *remain inseparable*.[12] I suspect that many theses about conscience are unacceptable because they neglect either the distinction or the interrelatedness of the two levels. The main stream of Scholasticism expressed the two levels of conscience by means of the concepts of *synderesis* and *conscientia*. The word *synderesis* (*synterêsis*) entered the medieval tradition of reflection on conscience from the Stoic reflection on the microcosm.[13] Since its precise meaning remained unclear, it prevented scholars from elaborating fully this essential level of the whole question of conscience. And this is why, without wishing to enter into the relevant debates within the field of intellectual history, I prefer to replace this problematic word by the much more clearly defined Platonic concept of anamnesis. This is linguistically clearer, and deeper and purer in philosophical terms. Besides, it is in harmony with fundamental motifs of biblical thinking and with the anthropology that is elaborated in the Bible.

The word "anamnesis" seeks here to affirm what Paul writes in his letter to the Romans: "When Gentiles who have not the law do by nature what the law requires, they are a law to themselves, even though they do not have the law. They show that what the law requires is written on their hearts, while their conscience also bears witness" (2:14–15).

We find an impressive formulation of the same idea in the great monastic rule of St. Basil: "The love of God is not based on some discipline imposed on us from outside, but as a capacity and indeed a necessity it is a constitutive element of our rational being." Basil uses an expression that was to become important in medieval mysticism when he speaks of the "spark of divine love that is innate in us."[14] In the spirit of

---

12. For a brief summary of the medieval doctrine of conscience, see Reiner, "Gewissen," 582f.

13. See E. von Ivánka, *Plato christianus* (Einsiedeln, 1964), 315–51, esp. 320f.

14. *Regulae fusius tractatae, Resp.* 2:1; PG 31:908.

Johannine theology, Basil knows that love consists in keeping the commandments. This is why the spark of love that we possess as creatures of God means the following: "We have received in advance the capacity and the willingness to carry out all the divine commandments.... They are not something imposed from outside ourselves." Augustine presents the simple core of this truth when he writes, "We would not be able to formulate the judgment that one thing is better than another unless a basic understanding of the good were imprinted upon us."[15]

Accordingly, the first level, which we might call the *ontological level,* of the phenomenon "conscience" means that a kind of *primal remembrance of the good and the true* (which are identical) is bestowed on us. There is an inherent existential tendency of man, who is created in the image of God, to tend toward that which is in keeping with God. Thanks to its origin, man's being is in harmony with some things but not with others. This anamnesis of our origin, resulting from the fact that our being is constitutively in keeping with God, is not a knowledge articulated in concepts, a treasure store of retrievable contents. It is an inner sense, a capacity for recognition, in such a way that the one addressed recognizes in himself an echo of what is said to him. If he does not hide from his own self, he comes to the insight: *this* is the goal toward which my whole being tends, *this* is where I want to go.

This *anamnesis of the Creator,* which *is identical with* the *foundations of our existence,* is the reason that *mission* is both *possible* and *justified.* The Gospel may and indeed must be proclaimed to the pagans, because this is what they are waiting for, even if they do not know this themselves (see Isa. 42:4). Mission is justified when those it addresses encounter the word of the Gospel and recognize that *this* is what they were waiting for. This is what Paul means when he says that the Gentiles

---

15. *De trinitate* 8.3:4; PL 42:949.

"are a law to themselves" — not in the sense of the modern liberalistic idea of autonomy, where nothing can be posited higher than the subject, but in the much deeper sense that nothing belongs to me *less* than my own self, and that my ego is the place where I must transcend myself most profoundly, the place where I am touched by my ultimate origin and goal. In this passage, Paul formulates his own experience as a missionary to the Gentiles, the same experience that Israel itself had already had in contact with the "God-fearers." In the Gentile world, Israel had encountered something that was confirmed anew in the experience of the messengers of Jesus Christ: their preaching responded to an expectation. It encountered a basic prior knowledge of the essential elements of the will of God that had taken written form in the commandments, and this knowledge is found in all cultures. This primal knowledge develops all the more purely where it is not distorted by the arrogance of "civilization." The more a person leads a life guided by the "fear of God" (see the story of the centurion Cornelius, especially Acts 10:34), the more concrete and clear will be the effect of this anamnesis.

Let us return to the formulation of St. Basil, the Doctor of the Church who insists that the love of God, which takes on specific form in the commandments, is not imposed on us from outside. Rather, it is infused into us a priori. "A basic understanding of the good is imprinted upon us," says Augustine. It is only on this basis that we can understand Newman's celebrated remark correctly, that if he were asked to make a religious toast he would indeed toast the pope, but he would toast conscience first. The pope does not have the power to impose commandments on believing Catholics just because he wants to do so or because he thinks it useful to do so. This modern voluntaristic concept of authority can only distort the true theological sense of the papacy. If the true essence of the Petrine ministry has become so incomprehensible in the modern period, this is surely because we can conceive of authority only on the basis of philosophical positions that exclude all bridges between subject and object. In such a view, whatever does not come from the subject can only be a heteronomous imposition.

If we start from the anthropology of conscience, which we have gradually attempted to explore in these reflections, the question must be posed in a completely different fashion. The anamnesis which is given to us and is inherent in our being needs help from outside in order that it may become aware of its own self. But this "outside" is not something opposed to the anamnesis. It exists in order to serve it. It has a maieutic function, not imposing something alien upon our anamnesis but activating something that is its own, activating the openness of the anamnesis to receive the truth.

In the case of faith and the Church, whose radius reaches from the redeeming Logos over the gift of Creation, we must however add a further level, which is developed with particular care in the Johannine writings. John knows the *anamnesis of the new "we"* that has been bestowed on us in our *incorporation into Christ*. We become one body, i.e., one "I" with him. The Gospel observes several times that the disciples came to understanding only subsequently, when they remembered. That first encounter with Jesus gave the disciples something that all generations now receive through their fundamental encounter with the Lord in baptism and the Eucharist: *the new anamnesis of faith* that, like the anamnesis of Creation, develops in the continuous dialogue between "inside" and "outside." This is why John could reply to the presumption of gnostic teachers, who wanted to persuade Christian believers that their naive faith ought to be understood and formulated in quite different terms, by saying, you do not need that kind of instruction, because as "anointed" (baptized) Christians you know everything (1 John 2:20). This does not mean that the faithful possess an intellectual knowledge of every single point of doctrine, but it does mean that Christian memory is unerring. It is always learning anew; its sacramental identity allows it to distinguish "from within" between that which assists the development of its memory and that which destroys or falsifies it.

In the crisis in today's Church we are experiencing afresh the power of this remembering and the truth of the apostolic word, where the power of the simple memory of the faith makes a much greater contribution to the discernment of spirits than do the directives issued by the hierarchy. It is only in this context that we can rightly understand papal primacy and its connection to the Christian conscience. The *true meaning of the teaching authority of the pope* is that he is the *advocate of Christian memory.* He does not impose something from the outside but develops and defends Christian memory. This is why the toast must quite rightly begin with conscience and then mention the pope, for *without conscience* there would be *no papacy* at all. All the power of the papacy is the power of conscience at the service of the double memory on which the faith is based and which must be continually assimilated anew, expanded, and defended against destruction of the memory. This memory is threatened both by a subjectivity that forgets the ground of its own being and by the pressure exerted by social and cultural conformity.

Conscientia

After these reflections on the first, essentially ontological, level of the concept of conscience, we must now turn to its second level, the only one to which the medieval tradition applied the term *conscientia*. It is likely that this terminological tradition made no little contribution to the shrinking of the concept of conscience in the modern period. Since Thomas applies the term only to this second level, it is logical that he sees conscience, not as a *habitus*, i.e., an abiding existential quality of man, but as an *actus*, i.e., an action that is performed. Naturally, Thomas presupposes the ontological basis of anamnesis (*synderesis*), which he describes as an internal contradiction of that which is evil and an internal orientation that we possess to the good. The act of conscience applies this basic knowledge in specific situations. According to Thomas, it consists of three elements: recognition (*recognoscere*), bearing witness (*testificari*), and finally judgment (*iudicare*). We might speak here of an interplay between the functions of control and of judgment.[16] On the basis of the Aristotelian tradition, Thomas understands this procedure on the model of the drawing of an inference, but he strongly underlines the specific character of this knowledge of what one ought to do: its conclusions are not inferred from knowledge or thinking alone.[17]

Whether something is recognized or not is always also *a question of the will,* which can *either block or open up the path to knowledge.* This depends therefore on an already existing moral formation that can be further perverted but can also be purified.[18]

It is true on this level of judgment (*conscientia* in the narrower sense) that an erring conscience obligates. The rational tradition of Scholasticism makes this proposition absolutely clear. As Paul had affirmed (Rom. 14:23), no one may act against his own convictions.[19] But the fact that one's

---

16. See Reiner, "Gewissen," 582; *S. theol.* I q 79 a 13; *De ver.* Q 17 a.

17. On this, see the careful study by L. Melina, *La conoscenza morale: Linee di riflessione sul Commento di san Tommaso all'Etica Nicomachea* (Rome, 1987), 69ff.

18. In the years following his conversion, Augustine reflected on his own inner experience and studied the connections between knowledge, the will, the emotional realm, and the effects of habit on the human personality. He arrived at fundamental insights into the essence of freedom and morality which deserve to be taken up afresh today. See the excellent study by P. Brown, *Augustine of Hippo* (London, 1967), 146–57.

19. The extremely illuminating study by J. G. Belmans, "Le paradoxe de la conscience erronée d'Abélard à Karl Rahner," *Revue Thomiste* 90 (1990), 570–86, shows that this is the precise position taken by Thomas Aquinas too. Belmans shows how Sertillanges's book on Thomas, which was published in 1942, pioneered a widespread but incorrect presentation of Thomas's doctrine of conscience, which consists — to simplify somewhat — in quoting only *S. theol.* I-II q 19 a 5 ("Must one follow an erring conscience?") while completely passing over the following article 6 ("Does it suffice to follow one's conscience, in order

conviction is naturally binding at the moment one acts does not mean a canonization of subjectivity. One who *follows the conviction* at which he has arrived, *never incurs guilt.* Indeed, one must follow such a conviction. But *guilt* may very well consist in *arriving at such perverse convictions* by trampling down the protest made by the anamnesis of one's true being. The *guilt* would then lie on a *deeper* level, not in the act itself, not in the specific judgment pronounced by conscience, but *in that neglect of my own being* that has dulled me to the voice of truth and made me deaf to what it says within me. And this is why criminals like Hitler and Stalin, who act out of deep personal conviction, remain guilty. Such grotesque examples are of course not meant to lull us into security about ourselves. They are meant to give us a shock that will bring home to us the seriousness of the prayer: "Clear thou me from hidden faults" (Ps. 19:12).

Epilogue: Conscience and Grace

We are left with our starting question: Is truth — at least, in the way the faith of the Church presents it to us — too lofty and difficult for human beings? After all our reflections, we can say that the steep path to truth, to the good, is not easy. It makes great demands of man. But remaining comfortably at home will not redeem us. That leads only to atrophy and the loss of our own selves. If we set out on the mountainous path to the good, we will discover more and more the beauty that lies in the efforts demanded by truth, and we will grasp that it is this that redeems us. However, this is not all there is to say. We would *dissolve Christianity into mere moralism if* we were to *fail* to present a *message* that *transcends our own*

to act well?"). This means attributing to Thomas the teaching of Abelard — although Thomas's goal was in fact to refute this! Abelard had taught that those who crucified Christ did not commit any sin, since they were acting out of ignorance; the only way to sin is to act against one's conscience. The modern theories of the autonomy of conscience can appeal to Abelard, but not to Thomas.

actions. We do not need a plethora of words to show this. We can see it in an image from the world that also indicates how the anamnesis of the Creator in us reaches out toward the Redeemer and how every man is able to comprehend that Christ is the Redeemer, because it is he who answers our innermost expectation. I have in mind the story of the expiation of Orestes, who had killed his mother. He had committed this murder as an act of conscience (the language of the myth calls this an act of obedience to the commandment of the god Apollo). But now he is hunted by the Erinyes, who are to be seen as mythical personifications of the conscience that torments him, out of a deeper memory, by objecting that his decision of conscience, his act of obedience to the "divine oracle," had in reality incurred guilt.

All man's tragedy becomes visible in this conflict between the "gods" in this contradiction of conscience. Before the sacred court, the white stone of Athene brings acquittal and sanctification to Orestes. The power of this sanctification changes the Erinyes to Eumenides, spirits of reconciliation, since expiation has transformed the world. This myth portrays more than just the transition from a system of blood-revenge to the ordered law of society, and Hans Urs von Balthasar expressed this extra dimension as follows: "The calming grace always assists in the establishing of justice, not the old graceless justice of the Erinyes period, but that which is full of grace."[20] This myth bears witness to a longing that the objectively correct verdict of guilt pronounced by the conscience and the resulting inner distress may not have the last word and that there may exist an authority of grace, a power of expiation, that removes the guilt and makes truth genuinely redemptive. This is a longing for a truth that does not merely make demands of us but is also a transforming expiation and

---

20. H. U. von Balthasar, *The Glory of the Lord: A Theological Aesthetics,* vol. 4, *The Realm of Metaphysics in Antiquity,* trans. Brian McNeil et al. (San Francisco: Ignatius Press, 1989), 121.

forgiveness, through which — as Aeschylus puts it — "guilt is washed off"[21] and our being is transformed from within, in a manner far exceeding our own powers. This is *the real novelty of Christianity: the Logos,* the Truth in person, *is also* this *expiation,* the *transforming forgiveness* that transcends all our own abilities and inabilities.

This is what is really new and on which the greater Christian memory is based, and that memory in turn is the deepest response for which the anamnesis of the Creator looks in us. *If we fail to see and proclaim this core of the Christian message clearly enough, truth will indeed become a yoke too heavy for our shoulders,* a yoke that we must try to throw off. But a freedom won in that manner would be empty, leading us into an utter wilderness, and such a freedom would disintegrate of its own accord. The yoke of truth became "light" (Matt. 11:30) when the Truth in person came, loved us, and burned up our guilt in his own love. It is only when we know and experience this from within that we become free to hear the message of conscience with joy — and without fear.

---

21. Aeschylus, *Eumenides* 280–81; see also von Balthasar, *Glory of the Lord.*

6

Searching for Peace

Tensions and Dangers

ɛ৶ɔ

When Allied troops began to disembark in German-occupied France on June 6, 1944, this was a signal to people throughout the world — and to many in Germany as well — that they were entitled to hope for an imminent peace and for freedom in Europe. What had happened? A criminal and his party followers had succeeded in seizing the power of the state in Germany, with the consequence that justice and injustice, law and crime, became entangled under the rule of the National Socialist Party. It was often virtually impossible to extricate one from the other, since a government headed by a criminal was also carrying out both the legislative and the administrative functions of the state. It was therefore in one sense entitled to demand that the citizens obey the law and respect the authority of the state (Rom. 13:1ff.!), while at the same time this government also employed the judicial organs as instruments in pursuit of its own criminal goals. The legal order itself continued to function in its usual forms in everyday lives, at least in part; at the same time, it had become a power that was used to undermine law. This perversion of orderly structures that were meant to promote justice but now consolidated the rule of injustice and made it virtually unassailable meant that people were governed by a lie that darkened their consciences. This rule of falsehood was served by a system of fear in which no one dared trust anyone else, because everyone had to protect himself in one way or another behind the mask of lies. While this did protect the individual, it made its own contribution to the consolidation of the power of evil.

The only way to shatter this cycle of crime and reestablish peace and the rule of law was an intervention by the whole world. In this hour, we express our thanks that this happened. This gratitude is felt not only by those countries that were occupied by German troops and thus handed over to Nazi terror. We Germans too are grateful that the committed action of the Allies restored our freedom and the rule of law. Here it is clear that the intervention of the Allies was a *bellum iustum*, a "just war," that ultimately served the good of those against whose country the war was waged. This is perhaps the clearest example in all history of a just war.

It seems to me important to note this point, because a real event in history shows that an absolute pacifism is untenable. Naturally, this does not dispense us from the task of formulating with great care the question whether, and under what circumstances, something like a "just war" is possible today, i.e., a military intervention against unjust systems of government that serves to promote peace and accepts the moral criteria for peace. I hope, however, that what I have said helps to make it clear that peace and law, peace and justice can never be separated from each other. Wherever law is destroyed, wherever injustice takes power, peace is put at risk, and indeed has already been damaged to some extent. Concern for peace is therefore first and foremost a concern to ensure a form of law that guarantees justice both for the individual and for society as a whole.

A Period of Peace Because of Shared Responsibility for the Rule of Law

Since the end of hostilities in May 1945, we have been given a period of peace in Europe longer than any other that our continent has seen at any time in its history. This is to no small degree the merit of the first generation of politicians in the postwar period — Churchill, Adenauer, Schumann, De Gasperi — whom we must thank today. They refused to be guided by the idea of retributive punishment, still less of revenge or the humiliation of the defeated. Rather, they wanted to do justice to everyone, replacing competition by collaboration, a mutual process of giving and receiving whereby the individual nations would get to know each other, cultivating friendship precisely in the variety of their own specific identities. Despite their diversity, these nations were all united in their shared responsibility for the rule of law after they had witnessed the perversion of law under Hitler. The core of this peacemaking politics was the link they made between political activity and morality. The inner criterion of all politics is those moral values that are not our own invention but that are discerned and are applicable to all men without distinction.

Let us state this point clearly: these politicians took their moral idea of the state, of law, of peace, and of responsibility from their Christian faith, which had been tested and tried in the Enlightenment and had been further purified in its opposition to the distortion of law and morality by the National Socialist Party. They did not want to construct a state based on faith but a state formed by ethical reason. Nevertheless, their faith had helped them to give new life to reason, which had been enslaved and disfigured by an ideological tyranny, and to reestablish the authority of reason. They conducted a politics of reason — of moral reason. Their Christianity had not estranged them from reason but had illuminated their reason.

We must of course add that a border ran through Europe, lacerating not only our continent but the entire world. Large sections of Central and Eastern Europe were under the domination of an ideology that made use of the party as its instrument and subordinated the state to the party, that is, made the state partisan. Here too, the consequence was the rule of falsehood and the destruction of mutual trust. After the collapse of these dictatorships, we have come to see the terrible economic, ideological, and psychological destruction that was wrought by their rule. Wars broke out in the Balkans, although of course ancient historical burdens also helped cause new explosions of violence there. If, however, we condemn the criminal dimension of those regimes and rejoice that they have been overthrown, we must still ask why most of the African and Asian peoples, the so-called nonaligned states, found the system in Eastern Europe more moral and a more realistic model for the structures of their own political life than the political and legal structures of the West. This certainly indicates deficits in our own structures, on which we must reflect.

Although Europe was permitted to experience a period of peace after 1945, with the exception of the conflicts in the Balkans, the situation of the world as a whole was anything but peaceful. From Korea to Vietnam, India, Pakistan, Bangladesh, Algeria, the Congo, Biafra/Nigeria, to the conflicts in Sudan, in Rwanda and Burundi, in Ethiopia, Somalia, Mozambique, Angola, Liberia, Afghanistan, and Chechnya, ran a bloody swath of warlike conflicts, to which we must add the fighting in and for the Holy Land and Iraq. This is not the place to examine the typology of these wars, whose wounds remain largely unhealed. I would however like to look more closely at two phenomena that are in one sense new, because they show us the specific risk of our own days and at the same time our own task in the search for peace.

THE DISSOLUTION OF LAW
AND OF THE CAPACITY FOR RECONCILIATION

The first phenomenon is the sudden collapse of law and of the ability to live together, which seems to be occurring in a number of societies. One typical example of the breakdown of the sustaining power of law, and thus of the decline into chaos and anarchy, is Somalia. But Liberia too shows how a society can dissolve from within because the authority of the state is incapable of presenting itself as a credible force for peace and freedom, with the result that everyone begins to try to establish his rights on his own. We experienced something similar in Europe after the united Yugoslavia broke up. Ethnic groups that had lived in peace with one another for many generations, despite the undeniable presence of tensions, were suddenly taking up weapons against one another with an incomprehensible cruelty. The dike of the soul was breached; protective forces were incapable of coping with the new situation, and the arsenal of hostility and of readiness to have recourse to violence, which had hitherto been kept in check by the forces of law and by a shared history, exploded in a terrible conflagration. It is of course true that different historical traditions lived alongside one another in that region, and there had always been latent tensions. The Latin and Greek forms of Christianity meet there, and the centuries of Turkish rule mean that Islam too is a living presence in the Balkans. And yet, despite all the tensions, there had existed a common life that now dissolved and gave way to anarchy.

How was this possible? Or how was it possible in Rwanda for the common life between Hutu and Tutsi to turn suddenly into bloody hatred? There are doubtless many causes for this breakdown of law and of the capacity for reconciliation, and we can identify some of them. In all these regions, the cynicism of ideology had darkened people's consciences. The *promises made by ideology* justified every instrument that appeared serviceable, thereby abolishing the distinction between good and evil. In addition to the *cynicism of ideology,* and often closely linked to it, there was the *cynicism of political interests and of big business,* the unscrupulous exploitation of the reserves of the earth. Here too the good is displaced by the useful, and power takes the place of law. In this way, the ethos of a people loses its power from within; and finally, even the utility that people seek is destroyed as well.

Here lies a great task for Christians today. We must learn the capacity for reconciliation with one another and do everything to ensure that conscience prevails and is not crushed by ideologies or partisan interests. In the Balkans (and by analogy in Northern Ireland) it must be the task of a genuine ecumenism to join in a common search for the peace of Christ, to give one another this peace, and to regard the ability to live in peace as a criterion of truth.

The Phenomenon of Terror

The other new phenomenon that oppresses us today is *terror*, which has become a new kind of world war — a war without clearly defined battle lines that can strike everywhere and no longer makes distinctions between combatants and the civilian population or between the guilty and the innocent. Since both terror and organized crime, which is spreading its net ever more widely and strongly, could conceivably get access to atomic and biological weapons, the peril that looms here is terrifying. As long as this potential for destruction lay in the hands of the superpowers alone, it was always possible to hope that reason and the awareness of the risks entailed for one's own people and state would prevent the use of these systems of weapons. As a matter of fact, we can thank God that we were spared a great war, despite all the tensions between East and West. In the case of forces of terror and organized criminal bands, however, we can no longer count on such rationality, because the willingness to destroy one's own life constitutes a basic element in the power of terrorism. This self-annihilation is declared to be a glorious martyrdom to which eschatological promises are attached.

In this situation, what can we do, and what ought we to do? Let us begin by noting some basic truths. It is impossible to overcome terrorism, illegal violence detached from morality, by force alone. It is indeed true that the defense of the rule of law against those who seek to destroy it must sometimes employ violence. This element of force must be precisely calculated, and its goal must always be the protection of the law. An absolute pacifism that refused to grant the law any effective means for its enforcement would be a capitulation to injustice. It would sanction the seizure of power by this injustice and would surrender the world to the dictatorship of force; we reflected briefly on this at the beginning of this essay. But in order that the force employed by law not itself become unjust, it must submit to strict criteria that are recognizable by all. It must pay heed to the causes of terrorism, which often has its source in injustices against which no effective action is taken. This is why the system of law must endeavor to use all available means to clear up any situations of injustice. Above all, it is important to contribute a measure of *forgiveness*, in order to break the cycle of violence. Where the principle of "an eye for an eye" is applied without pity, it is impossible to escape the power of that cycle. Gestures of a humanity that breaks through it by seeking the human person in one's foe and appealing to his humanity are necessary, even where they seem at first glance to be a waste of time.

In all these cases, it is important to prevent one single power from presenting itself as the guardian of the law, for it is all too easy for one-sided interests to come into play, making it harder to keep justice in view. An urgent requirement is a real *ius gentium*, a "law of nations," without disproportionate hegemonies and the actions to which these lead. Only so can it remain clear that the cause at stake is the protection of the rule of law on behalf of everyone, even of those who are fighting on the other side, so to speak. It was this that made the Second World War a convincing enterprise, and it was this that created a genuine peace between former enemies. What was at stake was not the extension of the rights of one side, but a common freedom and the genuine rule of law, although of course it was not possible to exclude altogether the emergence of new structures of hegemony.

In today's collision between the great democracies and the terrorism that finds its inspiration in Islam, however, even deeper questions are at stake. We seem to be witnessing a clash between two great cultural systems, the "West" and Islam, with very different forms of power and moral orientation. But what is the West? And who is Islam? These are multifaceted worlds, with tremendous internal differences — and these worlds overlap at many points. This means that the rough antithesis between the West and Islam is not satisfactory. Many are inclined to posit the true antithesis on a deeper level: on the one hand, we have enlightened reason, and on the other, a fundamentalist and fanatical form of religion. The primary task would then be to dismantle fundamentalism in all its forms and help win the victory for that reason which enlightened forms of religion permit.... The problem here, however, is that reason recognizes these forms of religion as "enlightened" precisely because they have submitted totally to the criteria proposed by this reason.

Highly Dangerous Pathologies in the Service of Peace

It is correct that in this situation the relationship between reason and religion is of crucial importance and that the heart of our striving for peace entails the endeavor to achieve the correct relationship between these two. I would like to offer a variation on some words of Hans Küng and say that *there cannot be world peace without the right peace between reason and faith*, because the springs from which morality and law draw dry up if there is no peace between reason and religion. Let me make my meaning clear by formulating the same idea in negative terms: as we see today, there exist pathologies of religion, as well as pathologies of reason. Both pathologies pose grave risks to peace and to humanity as a whole in our age with its global structures of power.

Let us look more closely at this point. God or the divine can turn into the absolutization of one's own power and one's own interests. A partisan image of God, which identifies the absoluteness of God with one's own community or its interests, thereby elevating something empirical and relative to a state of absoluteness, dissolves law and morality. The good now becomes whatever helps maintain one's own power; the real distinction between good and evil disintegrates. This is made even worse by the fact that the intention to act on behalf of one's cause is charged with a fanaticism centered on the absolute, a religious fanaticism, and thus becomes completely brutal and blind. God has become an idol in which human beings adore their own will. We see this in the terrorists' ideology of martyrdom, which of course in individual cases may also be the expression of despair at the lawlessness of the world. Sects in the Western world also provide examples of an irrationality and a perversion of religion that show how dangerous religion becomes when it loses its orientation.

But there also exists a pathology of reason that is completely detached from God, as we have seen in the totalitarian ideologies that parted company with God and wanted to construct the new man, the new world. We must certainly call Hitler an irrationalist; but the great preachers of Marxism and those who put its doctrines into practice certainly understood themselves as the builders of a world on the basis of reason alone. The most dramatic example of this pathology of reason is perhaps Pol Pot, under whom the cruelty of such a reconstruction of the world becomes appallingly clear. Even in the West, however, intellectual developments tend ever more toward destructive pathologies of reason. Was not the atomic bomb already a transgression of boundaries, where reason refused to be a constructive force but instead sought its strength in the ability to destroy? Now that reason is reaching for the very roots of life in its investigation of the genetic code, there is an increasing tendency to stop seeing man as a gift of the Creator (or of "nature") and to make him a product. Man is "made," and what one can "make" one can also unmake. Human dignity dissolves. And where are we then to find an anchor for human rights? How is respect for man — even the one who is conquered, weak, suffering, or handicapped — to survive?

All this blunts more and more the sharp contours of the concept of reason itself. In antiquity, for example, a distinction was made between *ratio* (reason in relation to the empirical, to the realm of what can be done), and *intellectus* (reason that contemplates the deeper strata of being). But all that remains now is *ratio* in the narrowest sense. Only that which is capable of verification — or more precisely, that which is capable of falsification — is now held to be rational. Reason reduces itself to those things that are open to experimental examination. All of morality and religion now belongs to the sphere of the "subjective," and this entire sphere has nothing to do with shared reason. Religion and morality do not fall within the province of reason; there are no longer any "objective" shared criteria of morality. In the case of religion, this outcome is considered unimportant, since each one will find his own path. In other words, religion is viewed as a kind of subjective ornamentation, which may perhaps possess a useful power to motivate certain people.

In the sphere of morality, some attempts are made to repair the damage. Naturally, if all of reality is merely the product of mechanical processes, it bears no kind of morality within itself. The good as such — still a central concern in a philosopher as late as Kant — no longer exists. A moral theologian, now deceased, once remarked that "good" means only "better than." If this is the case, nothing is intrinsically evil. The evaluation

of "good" and "evil" depends on a calculation of the consequences of one's acts. And that is in fact how the ideological
dictatorships behaved: if it helps the construction of the future
world of reason, it can on occasion be "good" to kill innocent
persons, who in any case no longer possess any absolute dignity. A sick reason and a misused religion thus lead in the end
to the same outcome. Sick reason ultimately regards as fundamentalism all knowledge of definitively valid values and every
insistence that reason is capable of discerning truth. The only
task remaining to sick reason is dissolution, deconstruction —
as we see in a writer like Jacques Derrida, who deconstructed
hospitality, democracy, the state, and finally even the concept
of terrorism, only to be left standing in shock at the events of
September 11, 2001. *Reason capable only of recognizing its
own self and that which is empirically certain paralyzes and
destroys itself.*

Faith in God, and the concept of God, can be misused and
become destructive. This is the threat to religion. But a reason that completely detaches itself from God, and is willing to
accept his existence only in the realm of the subjective, loses
its orientation, thereby opening the door to the powers of destruction. In the Enlightenment, people sought justifications
for morality that would be valid *etsi Deus non daretur*, "even if
God did not exist." Today, we must invite our agnostic friends
to be receptive to a morality *si Deus daretur*, "if God existed."
Kolakowski, with his experience of life in an atheistic-agnostic
society, has insistently demonstrated that without this absolute
point of reference, human conduct gets lost in indeterminacy
and becomes the hopeless prey of the forces of evil.[22] We Christians are summoned today, not to limit reason and oppose it,
but to resist its reduction to the rationality of production. We
must struggle on behalf of the capacity to perceive the good
and the good person, the holy and the holy person. For that is

---

22. See, e.g., L. Kolakowski, *Religion — If There Is No God* (New York, 1982).

the true fight on behalf of man and against inhumanity. Only reason that is open to God, only reason that does not banish morality into the realm of the subjective or degrade it to the level of calculations, can resist the misuse of the concept of God and sick forms of religion and bestow healing.

THE TASK OF CHRISTIANS

This indicates the great task that awaits Christians today. We must help reason to function in a comprehensive manner, not only in the spheres of technology and the material development of the world, but above all with regard to the capacity to perceive truth, the capacity to recognize the good, since the good is the precondition of law and thus also the presupposition of peace in the world. Our task as Christians today is to contribute our concept of God to the debate about man.

Two features characterize this concept of God. God himself is Logos, the rational primal ground of all that is real, the creative reason that gave birth to the world and that is reflected in the world. God is Logos — meaning, reason, and word, and that is why man corresponds to God when his reason is open and he pleads the cause of a reason that is not allowed to be blind to the moral dimensions of existence. For Logos designates a reason that is not merely mathematical: it is the basis of the good and guarantees the dignity of the good. Faith in the God who is Logos is at the same time faith in the creative power of reason. It is faith in the Creator God and faith that man is created in the likeness of God and therefore shares in the inviolable dignity of God himself. It is here that the idea of human rights finds its deepest foundations, although its historical development and elaboration have taken other paths.

God is Logos. We must add a second point: Christian faith in God also affirms that God, the eternal reason, is *love.* He is not a relationless existence circling around its own self. Precisely because he is sovereign, because he is the Creator and encompasses all things, he is relationship and love. Faith in the incarnation of God in Jesus Christ and in his suffering and dying for man is the highest expression of this conviction that the center of all morality, the center of existence itself and its innermost source, is love. This affirmation is the strongest possible rejection of every ideology of violence. It is the true *apologia* for man and for God. Nor should we forget that the God of reason and of love is also the judge of the world and of human beings, the *one who guarantees justice,* because everyone must give account to him. In view of the temptations to misuse power, it is fundamentally important for us not to forget the truth of judgment: everyone must give account of himself. There is a justice that is not simply abolished by love.

Plato's *Gorgias* contains a terrifying parable that is relevant here; it is not rendered obsolete by Christian faith; but rather it comes to its full validity in the Christian perspective. Plato says that the soul after death finally stands naked before the judge. Now the rank the soul held in the world is no longer relevant. It may be the soul of the king of Persia or of some other ruler. This does not matter, for the judge sees the traces left by perjury and by righteousness, the marks "that each of his deeds has imprinted upon the soul. And everything is twisted by falsehood and arrogance. He sees how the soul is weighed down by despotism, voluptuousness, presumption, and imprudence in action, extravagance, and baseness. . . . But sometimes he sees another soul standing before him, one that has led a pious and honest life, the soul of an ordinary citizen or a simple person. . . . Then the judge rejoices and sends it to the island of the blessed."[23] Where such convictions are strongly held, law and justice will be honored.

---

23. *Gorgias* 525A–526C.

A Common Moral Responsibility

I should like to mention a third element of the Christian tradition that is fundamentally important in the tribulations of our time. Thanks to the path taken by Jesus, Christian faith has dethroned the idea of a political theocracy. In modern terms, it has brought about the secularity of the state, in which Christians live together in freedom with members of other persuasions. They are bound together by the common moral responsibility that is based on the very essence of man, on the essence of justice. Christian faith distinguishes this reality from the kingdom of God, which does not and cannot exist in this world as a political entity. Its task is to transform the world from within by means of faith, hope, and love. Under the conditions of the present age, the kingdom of God is not a secular realm but an appeal addressed to human freedom and a support offered to reason so that it may fulfill its own task. In the last analysis, the temptations of Jesus concern this distinction, the rejection of political theocracy, the relativity of the state, and the right that properly belongs to reason. At the same time, they concern the freedom of that choice which every man must make.

In this sense, the lay state is a consequence of the fundamental Christian option, although it is true that a lengthy struggle was required before all the consequences of this option were understood. This secular, "lay" character of the state necessarily includes the balance between reason and religion that I have attempted to set out above. This character is of course also opposed to the ideology of laicism which would like to construct the state of pure reason, so to speak, cut loose from all historical roots and refusing to recognize any moral foundations except those that would win the assent of every person's reason. Ultimately, this laicism is left only with the positivism of the majority principle. And this means the ruin of law, which is thereby controlled by statistics.

Were the Western states to take this path completely, they would not be able in the long run to withstand the pressure of ideologies and political theocracies. Even a lay state may, and indeed must, find support in the dominant moral roots to which it owes its construction. It may and must acknowledge the basic values without which it would not have come into being and without which it cannot survive. *A state based on abstract, ahistorical reason has no future.*

In practical terms, this means that we Christians must join all our fellow citizens in elaborating a moral justification of law and of justice that is nourished by fundamental Christian insights, no matter how the individual would justify these and no matter how he connects them to the totality of his life. However, such shared rational convictions will be possible, and "right reason" will not forget how to see, only if we live our own inheritance vigorously and purely. This will make its inherent power of persuasion visible and effective in society as a whole.

I should like to conclude by quoting some words of Kurt Hübner, philosopher at the University of Kiel, that make this matter clear:

> The only way in which we shall ultimately avoid fighting against those cultures that are hostile to us today ... is to demonstrate the incorrectness of the passionate charge they level against us, that we have forgotten God. This requires us to become completely aware once more ... of the profound roots of our culture in Christianity. This will not suffice on its own to remove the resentment evoked by the superiority of the West in so many areas that dominate people's lives today, but it can make a significant contribution to the task of

quenching the religious embers that most enkindle this resentment.[24]

Hübner is perfectly correct. Without a new reflection on the God of the Bible, on the God who has drawn near in Jesus Christ, we shall not find the path that leads to freedom.

---

24. K. Hübner, *Das Christentum im Wettstreit der Weltreligionen* (Tübingen, 2003), 148.

7

What Must We Do?

Christians' Responsibility for Peace

ↄ

This day, June 6, 2004, is a day of remembrance. But remembrance does not only look to the past; it also seeks to give orientation for the future. Still, let us begin by looking to the past. Sixty years ago the great task was to liberate Europe and the world from a dictatorship that despised man: man was trampled upon, used, and misused in the service of a madness that wanted to create a new world. The ideology did indeed speak of God, but his name was only a label used to confer absoluteness on its own will. It was not the will of God that counted, but only the party's will for power. This meant that the image of God, before which we must stand in reverence, was no longer recognized in man. All that existed was the "human material" with which the ideology worked, but which it despised — just as in reality it despised God. An innumerable host of people were "used up" as material in the concentration camps, and a no less numerous host of young men died on the battlefields; we honor their graves today. We commend all the dead, no matter on which side they fought, to the mercy of God's kindness. They are all his children, each of them known, intended, and loved by God, each one called by his own name. Each one of them left behind a gap when he

died. Every single death called forth grief and pain. Now we
know that they are in the good hands of God, in his reconciling
kindness.

Every Man —
God's Image and Partner of Future Life

This presents us today with an occasion for reflecting anew
on the dignity of man, of each individual, as well as on death
and eternal life. We must learn to recognize God's image in all
men, no matter how alien or unattractive we may find them.
In each one we should also recognize a partner of our future
life, a person whom we will meet again when we leave this
world. And we should become newly conscious of our own
vocation to eternal life, living in such a way that we can one
day stand before the judgment seat of God with this present
life of ours.

In the generation to which I belong, the idea of a dimension beyond death and of eternal life has been pushed to the
margins, even in the Church's preaching. The suspicion that
Christians neglect life here on earth because they constantly
dream only of the life to come came to infect believing Christians themselves, including those who preached God's Word.
We were told that Christians shared only half-heartedly in the
work of constructing the world, which could have been better
and more humane long ago if only Christians had not practiced "flight from the world." Eternity can wait. The task now
is to make the earth a better place to live.

Well, these ideologies have not made it better and more humane. It is precisely the one who spends his days exercising
responsibility for eternal life who gives these days their full
weight. We see this in the parable of the talents: the Lord does
not summon us to a comfortable existence but to trade with
our talents (see Matt. 25:14–30). It is also true that one who
is aware of eternal life is liberated from the rapacious greed

that wants to enjoy everything to the full here and now, since he knows that the present age is the time for work and that the great feast comes afterward. The fields of death before which we stand admonish us to remember death and to lead our life aright in the face of eternity.

RECONCILIATION CREATES PEACE

When I recollect what it is that has brought us together here, three words occur to me: *reconciliation, peace, responsibility*. After the bloody conflicts of the Second World War, there began a process of reconciliation for which we can only be deeply grateful. By means of a generous aid program, America helped its former foe to rise anew from the ashes. Great Britain and France stretched out the hand of reconciliation to a country that had been their enemy in two world wars. Charles de Gaulle once said that it had been our obligation in the past to be each other's enemies, but now it was our joy to be able to be friends. This process of reconciliation, which was given to us in Europe and in the Atlantic partnership and was truly of world-historical dimensions, was born of a Christian spirit: only reconciliation creates peace. It is not violence that heals, but only justice. This must be the criterion of all political action in present-day conflicts.

The letter to the Hebrews speaks of the blood of Christ, which cries out in a different manner from the blood of Abel (12:24). It does not demand revenge but is reconciliation. The letter to the Ephesians makes the same point: Christ "is our peace." Through his death, "he has broken down the dividing wall of hostility that kept us apart." Through his blood, i.e., through his love that did not waver even in the face of death, he united those far off and those close at hand (see Eph. 2:14–22). It is this God that we preach, and it is this image of man that must guide us. The peace of Christ is not confined within the borders of Christendom but holds good for those far off just as much as for those close at hand. It is this peace that must determine the way we behave in small matters and in great.

This brings me to my third word: *responsibility*. In the aftermath of the First World War, and even more strongly after the Second, there arose a spontaneous cry: No more war! Sadly, reality looks different. The decades after 1945 have seen bloody wars in many regions of the world, and we must fear that injustice will raise its head again and again, and thus that it may again and again be necessary to defend law and justice against injustice, even by military means. What then may we hope for? And what must we do? The totalitarian ideologies of the twentieth century promised us that they would set up a liberated, just world — and they demanded hecatombs of victims in this cause. But the utopian image also influenced the Christian consciousness and left a deep impression on it. The expectation of Christ's return in glory points to a healing that lies beyond history, but men want a hope in history and for history. A fundamental term in the New Testament is the "kingdom of God," but many prefer to omit the word "God." They mention only the "kingdom," designating a new utopia that it is thought will captivate Christians and non-Christians alike. The "kingdom," the better world, is to be realized in history. Our faith does not promise us anything of the kind. In general, the recipes for the "kingdom" are so vague that they open the door to every ideological abuse. But, then, utopias and ideologies are a will-o'-the-wisp that leads people astray.

Strengthening the Forces of Good

Let us ask once more: What are we promised? What must we do? The Christian answer has three parts. First of all, we have the promise of the future Jerusalem, which is not made by man but comes from God.

Next, we have the prediction about the history of our world, that human freedom will continually be misused and that injustice will seize power again and again in the world. The Revelation of John paints frightening pictures of this reality, but the gloom of these pictures usually leads us to forget the other half, which is an essential dimension of the last book in the Bible: although God allows the freedom to choose evil considerable space in the world (too much space, we are often inclined to think), he never lets the world fall completely out of his hands. When the book of Revelation speaks of destruction, we encounter temporal limitations and what we might call percentages of ruin, "a third," for example. No matter what evil can do, the world belongs to God, not to evil, and this certainty is in fact a decisive part of the apocalyptic images. The author assumes that the terrors of which he writes are already known to Christians. His core affirmation is that these terrors will never have power over the whole world. They will never have the power to devastate it totally.

Finally, we have the third part of the Christian response to the question about the future, which is ethos and responsibility. There is no magic progress, no world correctly regulated once and for all, for that would be a world without freedom. God holds the world in his hands, but he does so to no small extent by means of our freedom, and we must use this — as a freedom to choose the good — to oppose the freedom of evil. Faith does not create a better world, but it does call forth and strengthen the freedom of the good against the temptation to misuse our freedom to do evil.

The commission that we receive from the graves of the Second World War is to strengthen the forces of good and to plead, work, live, and suffer for those values and truths that hold the world together under God. God promised Abraham that he would not destroy the city of Sodom if ten righteous men were found there (Gen. 18:32). We ought to do all we can to ensure that the ten righteous ones who can save a city are never lacking.

8

Acting in the Strength That Comes from Remembrance

The Grace of Reconciliation

 cs

In this hour, at the German military cemetery at La Cambe near Caen, we reverently bow before the dead of the Second World War and remember the many young men from our country whose future and hope perished in the bloody battles of the war. As Germans, we must be painfully moved by the way in which their idealism and their obedience to the state were misused by an unjust regime. But this does not lessen the honor due to these young men; only God can see their consciences. And each one stands alone before God with the path he took in his life and with his dying. We know that all our dead are kept safe in the merciful kindness of God. They attempted quite simply to do their duty, often with terrible inner conflicts, doubts, and questions. Now they look at us and speak to us: What about you? What are you going to do to prevent young men from being driven again into such battles? What are you going to do to prevent the world from being laid waste anew by hatred and violence and falsehood?

United in a New Solidarity

This is a time for grief and for the examination of our consciences, but it is also a time for profound gratitude, since reconciliation has grown over these graves. Foes have become friends, taking each other's hands so that they may walk together. Even from within the perspective of history, the sacrifice of our dead was not in vain. After the First World War, the enmity and bitterness remained alive between the warring nations, especially between Germany and France, poisoning people's souls. The Treaty of Versailles deliberately set out to humiliate Germany, imposing burdens that radicalized people and thereby opened the door to Hitler's dictatorship. The treaty created a ready audience for the lying promises to restore the freedom, honor, and greatness of Germany. An eye for an eye, a tooth for a tooth — we have seen that this principle does not lead to peace.

Thank God, things were different after the Second World War. With the Marshall Plan the Americans gave generous aid to us Germans so that we could rebuild our country, and they made a new prosperity and freedom possible. In the new global constellation, with the collapse of the colonial empires and the confrontation between East and West, people at once became aware that only a united Europe can have a voice in the progress of history and that the nationalisms that had torn our continent apart must cease and be replaced by a new solidarity. And thus, after the conflicts that had etched their bloody traces on so many centuries, an ever closer friendship grew between Germany and France. Europe has grown in widening circles since the 1950s, and today we stand as reconciled friends before the graves that remind us of our battles of the past.

In this hour, as we look back, the continuing process of reconciliation and of mutual solidarity seems to us completely logical, indeed something demanded by the new constellations of world history. But we should not overlook the fact that this logic did not immediately convince everyone. Its success was not automatic. History shows us how often people have acted against logic and reason. The victory of the policy of reconciliation is the contribution of a generation of politicians represented by names such as Adenauer, Schumann, De Gasperi, and de Gaulle. They possessed a sober understanding and political realism, but this realism stood on the solid ground of the Christian ethos, which they recognized as the ethos of purified reason. They knew that politics is more than a mere pragmatism. It must always be a moral matter, since the goal of politics is justice accompanied by peace, and it employs the criteria of law to regulate the exercise of power. If the essence of politics is the moral ordering of power on the basis of the criteria provided by law, then the heart of politics is one of the fundamental categories of morality.

Rooted in the Values of Christian Faith

But where and how are we to find the criteria for justice? These men did not doubt that the fundamental directives for the establishing of justice, valid for all times, were to be found in the Ten Commandments, which they read in the continuation and deepening that these words received in the message of Christ. The emergence of Europe after the collapse of the Greco-Roman world and the mass migration of peoples was the work of Christianity. It is indisputable that it was Christian faith that give birth to Europe in that period. In the same way, the restoration of Europe after the Second World War has Christianity as its root, and this means that it has responsibility before God as its root. After the perversions of the law under the Nazi regime, the German constitution very consciously declared this responsibility before God to be the deepest anchor of our country as a state under the rule of law.

If we wish to build up Europe today as a stronghold of law and of justice vis-à-vis all men and cultures, we cannot withdraw to an abstract reason that knows nothing of God, a reason that itself belongs to no culture but wants to regulate every culture according to its own criteria — for what criteria are they? What freedom can such a reason grant or withhold? Even today, responsibility before God and rootedness in the great values and truths of Christian faith, which unite all the various confessions, provide the essential forces for the construction of a Europe that is more than an economic bloc. It is to be a community of law, a stronghold of law — not only for itself, but for mankind as a whole.

The dead of La Cambe speak to us. They are at peace. But they ask us: What are you doing for peace? They warn us against a state that loses the foundations of law, that cuts off its own roots. The remembrance of the injustice of the Second World War and of the great history of reconciliation that followed it in Europe shows us where to find the powers that heal. It is only when we allow God to enter the world that the earth can become whole and the world become humane.

PART
III

WHAT IS EUROPE?

Foundations and Perspectives

❧

9

Europe's Identity

Its Intellectual Foundations
Yesterday, Today, and Tomorrow

☙

What is "Europe"? Cardinal Glemp kept on asking this question in one of the linguistic discussion groups at the Synod of Bishops that was held in Rome on the subject of Europe: Where does Europe begin, and where does it end? Why, for example, is Siberia not a part of Europe, although most of its inhabitants are Europeans who think and live in a thoroughly European manner? And where does Europe end in the southern regions of the former Soviet Union? Where is its border in the Atlantic? Which islands form part of Europe, which do not — and why not? These conversations made it completely clear that it is only in a secondary sense that "Europe" is a geographical concept: Europe is not a continent with clear geographical boundaries but a cultural and historical concept.

THE EMERGENCE OF EUROPE

This becomes very obvious when we attempt to get back to the origins of Europe. Discussions of these origins usually point to Herodotus (ca. 484–425 BC), who was probably the first to possess a geographical concept of Europe, which he defines as

129

follows: "The Persians regard Asia with its peoples as their land. They believe that Europe and the land of the Greeks lie completely outside their own borders."[1] He does not indicate the borders of Europe itself, but it is clear that central regions in today's Europe lay altogether outside the area he had in mind. The development of the Hellenistic cities and of the Roman Empire led to the formation of a "continent" on which the later "Europe" was based, although with completely different boundaries. It consisted of the lands around the Mediterranean that formed a genuine "continent" through their cultural links, through travel and trade, and through a common political system. It was only the military victories of Islam in the seventh and early eighth centuries that drew a border through the Mediterranean, slicing across it in such a way that what had formerly been one continent now split into three: Asia, Africa, and Europe.

In the East, the reshaping of the world of antiquity was a slower process than in the West. The Roman Empire, with Constantinople as its heart, was forced to abandon more and more territory, but nevertheless survived into the fifteenth century.[2] Around 700 the southern shores of the Mediterranean definitively parted company with the cultural continent that had existed hitherto. At the same period, however, there was an ever-stronger expansion in a northerly direction. The *limes*, which had been the boundary of a continent until then, disappeared, and a historically important new region came into being with Gaul, Germany, and Britain as its heartlands. This region increasingly came into contact with Scandinavia too. As the borders shifted, the intellectual continuity with the earlier Mediterranean continent, which had occupied a different

---

1. Herodotus, *Histories,* ed. Josef Feix (Munich, 1995), 1.
2. For a broad overview of the shaping of Europe in terms of geography and of values, see Peter Brown, *Divergent Christendoms: The Emergence of a Christian Europe, 200–1000 AD*, 8th ed. (Oxford, 1995).

geographical region, was preserved by means of a hypothesis drawn from the theology of history. Following the book of Daniel, the Roman Empire, which had been renewed and transformed by Christian faith, was understood to be the final and lasting empire of world history, so that the structure of peoples and states that was now coming into being was defined as the abiding *Sacrum Imperium Romanum*.

This process of a new historical and cultural identification was carried out very consciously under Charlemagne, and it is here that the old word "Europe" is used again, but with a new meaning. It now designates the empire of Charlemagne and expresses the consciousness of continuity and the newness that demonstrated that the new state would dominate future history — precisely because it understood itself as anchored in a continuity with previous history and, ultimately, in that which is eternal.[3] This emerging self-understanding expressed an awareness that something definitive had occurred and an awareness of a mission. It is true that after the end of the Carolingian empire, the concept of Europe largely disappeared and was confined to the language of scholars. It entered the popular vocabulary only at the beginning of the modern period, probably as a means of self-identification in the context of the danger posed by the Turks, and won universal acceptance in the eighteenth century. Independently of this history of the word itself, the constitution of the Frankish kingdom as the Roman Empire, which had never actually perished and was now born anew, was the decisive step toward the reality we mean today when we speak of Europe.[4]

Of course, we must remember that Europe has a second root, which is not Western or occidental. As I have mentioned, the Roman Empire in Byzantium survived the storms of the

---

3. See H. Gollwitzer, "Europa, Abendland," in *Historisches Wörterbuch der Philosophie,* ed. J. Ritter, II, cols. 824–26; F. Prinz, *Von Konstantin zu Karl dem Großen* (Düsseldorf, 2000).
4. See Gollwitzer, "Europa, Abendland," col. 826.

mass migration of peoples and the Islamic invasion. Byzantium understood itself as the real Rome. Here, the Roman Empire had in fact survived, and this is why Byzantium continued to lay claim to the western half of that empire. This eastern Roman Empire also experienced a wide expansion northward, into the Slavic world, creating a Greco-Roman world of its own, which differed from the Latin Europe of the West in its liturgy, church order, and alphabet, and in its refusal to employ Latin as the common language of education.

At the same time, there were sufficient elements uniting the two worlds so that they could still form one common continent. First of all, there was the shared inheritance of the Bible and the early Church, which pointed in both worlds to an origin that now lay outside "Europe," that is, in Palestine. There was also the same idea of the empire and the same basic ecclesiology and, hence, also common ideas of jurisprudence and common legal instruments. Finally I should like to mention monasticism, which remained the great upholder not only of cultural continuity in the tremendous storms of history but also of those basic religious and ethical values that provide the ultimate orientations for human life. As a force lying outside and above politics, monasticism provided again and again the impetus for a necessary rebirth of society.[5]

Despite the fact that both Europes shared this basic ecclesial patrimony, however, there also existed a profound difference, to which Endre von Ivánka has drawn attention. In Byzantium, the empire and the Church were virtually identified with each other, and the emperor was also the head of the Church. He understood himself as the vicar of Christ and bore the official title "king and priest" from the sixth century onward, following the example of Melchizedek, who was both king

---

5. There is a vast secondary literature on monasticism; I mention here only H. Fischer, *Die Geburt der westlichen Zivilisation aus dem Geist des romanischen Mönchtums* (Munich, 1969); F. Prinz, *Aszese und Kultur Vor- und frühbenediktinisches Mönchtum an der Wiege Europas* (Munich, 1980).

and priest (Gen. 14:18).[6] After Constantine left Rome and the emperors no longer resided in the earlier imperial capital, it was possible for the autonomous position of the bishop of Rome as successor of Peter and head of the Church to develop there, and the doctrine of a dual authority was taught in Rome from the beginning of the Constantinian epoch. The emperor and the pope each had an authority of his own, and neither of them possessed the totality of power. Pope Gelasius I (492–496) formulated the Western view in his famous letter to Emperor Anastasius, and even more clearly in his fourth treatise, in which he responds to the Byzantine use of the typology of Melchizedek by emphasizing that it is only in Christ that the two authorities are united: "It is Christ himself, because of human weakness (*superbia!*), who separated the two offices for the subsequent ages, so that no one might exalt himself" (chap. 11). The Christian emperors require the priests (*pontifices*) for things pertaining to eternal life. In turn, the priests adhere to the ordinances promulgated by the emperor for the temporal course of affairs. In secular matters the priests must follow the laws of the emperor, who is installed in office by God's decree, but in divine matters the emperor must submit to the priests.[7]

---

6. F. von Ivánka, *Rhomäerreich und Gottesvolk* (Freiburg and Munich, 1968).

7. For textual references and secondary literature, see U. Duchrow, *Christenheit und Weltverantwortung* (Stuttgart, 1970), 328ff. Hugo Rahner, *Kirche und Staat im frühen Christentum* (Munich, 1961), presents a wealth of relevant material. S. Horn has drawn my attention to an important text by Leo the Great, a passage in the letter sent by the pope to the emperor on May 22, 452, in which he rejects the decree later known as canon 28 of Chalcedon (which accorded primacy to Constantinople alongside Rome, since it was the residence of the emperor): *Habeat sicut optamus Constantinopolitana civitas gloriam suam, et protegente Dei dextera diuturno clementiae vestrae fruatur imperio, alia tamen ratio est rerum saecularium alia divinarum, nec praeter illam petram quam Dominus in fundamento posuit stabilis erit constructio* ("Let the city of Constantinople, in accordance with our own wish, have its own glory, and may it long enjoy the rule of your clemency, under the protection of God's right hand; but the ordering of secular matters is one thing, and the ordering of divine matters another, nor will the construction be stable without that rock which the Lord himself placed in its foundation"; LME II [37] 55:52–56; see also ACO II/IV, p. 56). On this question, see also A. Michel, "Der Kampf um das politische oder petrinische Prinzip der

This introduced a separation and distinction of powers that was to be immensely important for the subsequent development of Europe, laying the foundations of that which is typically Western. Since such demarcations did not suppress the desire on both sides to possess the totality of power or the yearning to subordinate the other side to its own authority, this principle of separation was also the source of unending suffering. A basic problem confronting Europe today and tomorrow is how we can create the right structures for this separation and what political and religious forms it should take.

THE BREACH IN CONTINUITY
AT THE BEGINNING OF THE MODERN PERIOD

These observations allow us to regard the emergence of the Carolingian realm, on the one hand, and the continued existence of the Roman Empire in Byzantium and its Slavic mission, on the other hand, as the real birth of the European "continent." The beginning of the modern period brought a breach in continuity for both Europes, affecting both the essence of this continent and its geographical borders. In 1453, Constantinople was conquered by the Turks. O. Hiltbrunner comments laconically: "The last ... scholars emigrated ... to Italy and imparted the knowledge of the Greek original texts to the Renaissance humanists; but the East sank down into a cultureless torpor."[8] This formulation may be somewhat harsh, since the Ottoman Empire too had its own culture, but it is correct to say that this was the end of the Christian Greek, "European" culture of Byzantium.

Kirchenführung," in *Das Konzil von Chalkedon*, ed. A. Grillmeier and H. Bacht, vol. II: *Entscheidung um Chalkedon* (Würzburg, 1953), 491–562, and the article by Thomas O. Martin about canon 28 of Chalcedon in the same volume, 433–58.

8. In *Kleines Lexikon der Antike* (Munich, 1950), 102.

Although one wing of Europe was threatened with extinction, the Byzantine inheritance was not dead. Moscow declared itself the third Rome and now founded a patriarchate of its own on the basis of the idea of a second "transfer of the empire." It now presented itself as a new metamorphosis of the *Sacrum Imperium* — as a specific form of Europe that remained linked to the West and increasingly found its orientation there, until finally Peter the Great attempted to make Russia a Western country. This northward transposition of Byzantine Europe also meant that its borders were extended far to the East. Although the definition of the Urals as the boundary is completely arbitrary, the world to the east of those mountains became more and more a kind of "outbuilding" of Europe, neither Asia nor Europe. Europe was the subject that formed this region, which was not allowed to share in the character of "subject." It remained an object, not the author of its own history. And perhaps that is the basic definition of colonial status.

We can therefore speak of a double transition in Byzantine, non-Western Europe at the start of the modern period. On the one hand, the old Byzantium with its historical continuity with the Roman Empire is extinguished, and on the other hand, this second Europe finds a new center in Moscow and extends its borders eastward until it sets up a kind of colonial porch in Siberia. In the same period, we can observe a double transition in the West with far-reaching historical consequences. A large portion of the Germanic world separated from Rome, and a new, "enlightened" kind of Christianity emerged, so that a border now ran through the "West," which clearly also constituted a cultural *limes* separating two different modes of thought and conduct. Naturally, there were fissures within the Protestant world too, between Lutherans and Reformed, to say nothing of Methodists and Presbyterians, and the Anglican Church attempted to develop a middle path between Catholicism and Protestantism. To this we must add the difference between a Christianity that took the form of state churches (typical of Europe) and the free churches that found their place of refuge in America. We shall return to this point.

Let us first note the second process that fundamentally transformed the situation of formerly Latin Europe in the modern period, the discovery of America. Europe expanded eastward through the continuous extension of Russia into Asia. In the same way, Europe broke radically with its geographical boundaries and entered the world beyond the ocean, which was now given the name "America." The separation of Europe into a Latin Catholic half and a Germanic Protestant half was transposed to this continent, to which Europe now laid claim. Initially, America too was an extended Europe, a "colony," but it acquired its own character as a subject when Europe's foundations were rocked by the French Revolution. From the nineteenth century onward, America acted toward Europe as its own subject, although one that remained deeply marked by its European birth.

In our attempt to discern the inner identity of Europe by looking at its history, we have now seen *two fundamental historical upheavals*. First, there was the replacement of the old Mediterranean continent by the continent of the *Sacrum Imperium*, which lay further to the north, in which "Europe" came into being from the Carolingian epoch onward as the Western Latin world. At the same time, the old Rome continued to exist in Byzantium and extended into the Slavic world. We observed the second step in the fall of Byzantium, leading to the transposition of the Christian imperial idea northward and eastward on the one flank of Europe, while on the other flank we noted the internal division of Europe into a Germanic Protestant and a Latin Catholic world. When Europeans reached America, they brought this division with them. Finally, America was constituted as a specific historical subject vis-à-vis Europe.

The French Revolution raised the banner of a third up-heaval, which became visible far and wide, and we must now look at this. The *Sacrum Imperium* had been in decline as a political reality since the late Middle Ages, and the interpretation of history that it represented had become increasingly brittle. But it was only now that this intellectual framework, without which Europe could never have come into existence, actually collapsed. In terms both of politics and of the history of ideas, this was an exceedingly important event. It meant the rejection of a divine foundation for history and the existence of the state. History is no longer subject to the criterion of an antecedent idea of God that gives it its form, and the state is now considered in purely secular terms as an entity based on rationality and on the will of its citizens. For the very first time in history, we see a purely secular state that discards, as a mythical world view, the idea that God is the ultimate guarantor of political life and that it is he who lays down the norms for its conduct. This state declares God himself to be a private matter that has no place in the public sphere in which the shared will of the citizens is formed. This sphere is now considered a matter of reason alone, and reason cannot clearly recognize God. Religion and faith in God belong to the realm of the emotions, not to that of reason. God and his will lose their relevance to public life.

In this way, a new kind of division in faith arises at the end of the eighteenth and the beginning of the nineteenth centuries, and we are now coming increasingly to feel its full seriousness. In the Romance languages, this is described as a division between the "Christian" and the "lay" world view. In the last two centuries, it has created a deep fissure in the Latin nations, whereas Protestant Christianity initially found it easier to accommodate liberal and Enlightenment ideas without shattering the framework of a broad basic Christian consensus. This is why there is no German noun to designate this division, which has taken a longer time to produce its effects in our countries.

In the political sphere, the demise of the ancient imperial idea means that it is now definitively the nations — recognizable as such thanks to the development of unified linguistic regions — that are the only real actors in history, thus acquiring a rank they had not had before. The explosive dramatic potential of this historical subject, which now takes a plural form, lies in the fact that the great European nations believed that a historical mission had been entrusted to them. This necessarily had to lead to a conflict between these nations, and we have witnessed the lethal impact of this conflict in the sufferings of the twentieth century.

THE UNIVERSALIZATION OF EUROPEAN CULTURE AND ITS CRISIS

Finally, we must note one further process that takes the history of the last centuries into a new epoch. The two halves of the old Europe before the modern period had known only *one* other reality with which they faced a life-and-death confrontation, namely, the Islamic world. The upheaval in the modern period had brought expansion to America and to parts of Asia where there were no significant cultural subjects. Now, however, Europe reached out to the two continents with which it had had only marginal contacts hitherto, Africa and Asia, and the attempt was made to transform these into offshoots of Europe, into "colonies." To some extent this was in fact successful. Asia and Africa too are keen to follow the ideal of a world of technology and to have the prosperity this brings, with the result that ancient religious traditions have entered a period of crisis there too, and public life is dominated more and more by groups who think in purely secular terms.

We can, however, note a movement in the other direction. The renaissance of Islam is not only linked to the new material wealth of Islamic countries but is also born of the conviction that Islam can offer a solid intellectual basis for the life of the peoples. The old Europe seems to have lost this basis, and it is held to be doomed to decline and to disappear, despite its continuing political and economic power. The great religious traditions of Asia, above all Buddhism, which gives expression to its mystical component, are rising up as intellectual forces against a Europe that denies its religious and ethical foundations. At the beginning of the 1960s it was still possible for Arnold Toynbee to express his optimism about the victory of European culture. He wrote that of the twenty-eight cultures that had been identified, eighteen were already dead; and of the ten that still existed, nine had already visibly collapsed, so that only one — ours, the European — remained.[9] Who would dare to say that today? And what is "our" culture, which allegedly still remains? Is the civilization of technology and commerce that has spread victoriously throughout the world our "European culture"? Or is it not something born in the post-European age, the outcome of the end of the old European cultures? I see a paradoxical synchronicity here: the victory of the post-European technical-secular world and the universalization of its pattern of life and its way of thought are accompanied throughout the world, but especially in the highly non-European worlds of Asia and Africa, by the impression that the world of Europe's values, its culture and its faith that are the basis of its identity, has in fact already disappeared from the scene and that the hour of the value systems of other worlds — of pre-Columbian America, of Islam, of Asian mysticism — has now come. In the very hour of its most extreme success, Europe seems to have become empty from

---

9. A. J. Toynbee, *A Study of History*, abridged ed. (Oxford, 1987). See also J. Holdt, *Hugo Rahner: Sein geschichtstheologisches Denken* (Paderborn, 1997), 53; the section "Philosophische Besinnung auf das Abendland" (52–61) offers important material on the question of Europe.

within. Its life seems threatened by a crisis of circulation, and it almost seems to need a transfusion of blood — but that would destroy its own identity. In keeping with this dying of the elemental forces that expressed the soul, the reduced number of births makes one suspect that Europe is also dying out in ethnic terms.

There is a remarkable reluctance to embrace the future. Children, who are the future, become a threat to the present day, and people feel that children take away something from our life. They are often seen, not as a hope, but rather as a restriction. There is an obvious parallel here to the Roman Empire in the days of its decline: it continued to function as a huge historical framework, but its own existential vigor was dead, and it already lived thanks only to those who in fact wanted to destroy it.

This brings us to the problems of our own time. There are two antithetical diagnoses of the future that may await Europe. We have the thesis of Oswald Spengler, who believed that one could observe a kind of natural course of history for great cultural structures: there is the moment of birth, the gradual ascent, the flourishing of a culture, the slow process whereby it becomes tired and old, and its death. Spengler offers impressive evidence in support of his thesis from the history of those cultures in which this regular course of events can be demonstrated. His thesis was that the West had now arrived in its late phase, which, despite all protestations to the contrary, would ineluctably lead to the death of this cultural continent. Naturally, Europe can hand on its gifts to a newly ascendant culture, as happened in the case of earlier cultural deaths, but as a subject its days are numbered.

Between the two world wars, this thesis was criticized as biologistic, and it was passionately opposed, especially by Catholic writers. Arnold Toynbee too took up cudgels against it in an impressive fashion, though with arguments that few today find convincing.[10] Toynbee emphasizes the difference between material and technological progress, on the one hand, and genuine progress, which he calls spiritualization, on the other. He concedes that the "Western world" is in a crisis, and he identifies its roots in the falling away from religion to embrace a cult of technology, of the nation, and of militarism. Ultimately, he identifies the crisis as secularism. But if we can name the cause of the crisis, we can also indicate the path to healing: the religious element must be reintroduced. Toynbee holds that this element includes the religious patrimony of all cultures, but especially what remains of Western Christianity.[11] He responds to the biologistic view with a voluntaristic understanding that relies on the vigor of creative minorities and outstanding individual personalities.

We must ask whether this diagnosis is correct and, if so, whether it lies in our power to reintroduce the religious element in a synthesis between the remnants of Christianity and the religious inheritance of mankind. Ultimately, the question debated by Spengler and Toynbee remains open, because we cannot look into the future. Quite apart from this, however, we must ask where we can find a future and what can maintain the internal identity of Europe through all the metamorphoses of history. We can put it even more simply: What is likely to guarantee human dignity, and a life in keeping with this dignity, today and tomorrow?

To answer this question, we must once again look at the present time, while bearing in mind its historical roots.

---

10. O. Spengler, *Der Untergang des Abendlandes*, 2 vols., 1st ed. (Munich, 1918–22). On the debates that his thesis kindled, see the chapter "Die abendländische Bewegung zwischen den Weltkriegen" in Holdt, *Hugo Rahner*, 13–17. The debate with Spengler is a leitmotif in a fundamental work of moral philosophy in the period between the wars: T. Steinbüchel, *Die philosophische Grundlegung der katholischen Sittenlehre*, 2 vols. (Düsseldorf, 1st ed., 1938; 3rd ed., 1947).
11. See Holdt, *Hugo Rahner*, 54.

Our reflections paused at the French Revolution and the nineteenth century. In the intervening period, two new "European" models developed. In the Latin nations, we find the "laicist" model, where the state is strictly separate from religious bodies, which belong to the private sphere. The state itself rejects any religious basis and is founded on reason alone and the insights that this imparts. Thanks to the fragility of reason, these systems have proved precarious and an easy prey for dictators. The only reason for their survival is the continued existence of parts of the old moral awareness even when the previous foundations are removed. It is this that makes a basic moral consensus possible.

On the other hand, we find various models in the Germanic regions of the liberal Protestant state church, in which an "enlightened" Christian religion, which is basically understood as morality, guarantees the moral consensus and a religious foundation to society, understood in broad terms. The forms of worship are also approved by the state. Religions that are not themselves the state church must adapt to the religious foundation that the state church supplies. For a long time, this model guaranteed the cohesion of the state and of society in Great Britain, in the Scandinavian states, and in Germany under Prussian domination. In Germany, however, the collapse of the Prussian state church system left a vacuum that the Nazi dictatorship all too easily filled. Today, all the surviving state churches suffer from anemia. No moral force emanates from religious bodies that owe their existence to the state, since the state itself cannot create any moral force. It must presuppose this and build on it.

Between these two models, we have the United States of America. On the one hand, thanks to the central historical role of the free churches, the starting point here is a strict dogma of the separation of church and state. On the other hand, the individual denominations worked together to create a basic

Protestant Christian consensus not bound to any one particular confession, and this has left a deep imprint on the United States. This is linked to a particular consciousness of mission to the rest of the world, thus endowing the religious element with a significant weight in public life: this has been a prepolitical and suprapolitical force that exercised a determinative influence on political life. Naturally, it is obvious that the Christian heritage is dissolving rapidly in America too. At the same time, the influx of Spanish-speaking people and the presence of religious traditions from the whole world are altering the picture. We ought perhaps to note here that the United States is clearly promoting the Protestantization of Latin America, on the basis of a conviction that the Catholic Church cannot guarantee stable economic and political systems and thus is failing to do its duty as teacher of the nations. The aim is to replace the Catholic Church by free-church forms of religion, in the expectation that this model will make possible in Latin America the same kind of moral consensus and construction of democratic will that are characteristic of the United States. The picture is further complicated by the fact that the Catholic Church is the largest religious body in the United States today and that it most decidedly holds to its Catholic identity. However, Catholics have adopted the free-church traditions regarding the relationship between the church and politics, in the sense that a church that is not merged with the state is a better guarantee of the moral foundations of society as a whole. This means that the promotion of the democratic ideal is seen as a moral obligation deeply consonant with the faith. We are justified in seeing such a position as a contemporary continuation of the model of Pope Gelasius, which I mentioned above.

Let us return to Europe. The two models that we have discussed were complemented in the nineteenth century by a third, namely, socialism, which soon split into two tendencies, the totalitarian and the democratic. Thanks to its starting point, democratic socialism has proved to be a healthy counter-weight to radical liberal positions and has been integrated into the two existing models, enriching them and also correcting them. It was able to transcend confessional divisions. In England, it was the party of the Catholics, who did not feel at home in either the Protestant Conservative party or the Liberal camp. In Germany under Wilhelm II, the Catholic Center party often felt more akin to democratic socialism than to the strictly Prussian conservative Protestants. On many points, democratic socialism has been and remains close to Catholic social doctrine, and it has at any rate made a considerable contribution to the creation of a social consciousness.

The totalitarian model joined arms with a strictly materialistic and atheistic philosophy of history that understood history deterministically, as a process of progress via religious and liberal phases toward the absolute and definitive society; religion would be superseded as a remnant of the past and the functioning of material conditions would ensure universal happiness. Its apparently scientific character conceals an intolerant dogmatism: the spirit is a product of matter, and morality is a product of circumstances that is to be defined and practiced in accordance with the goals of society. Everything that serves to bring nearer the happy final state of things is "moral." This is a complete reversal of those values that had built Europe. Even worse, it is a rupture with the entire moral tradition of mankind. There are no longer any values independent of the goals of progress, and everything can be permissible or even necessary — moral, in the new sense of the term — in a given situation. Even man can become a means to an end. It is not the individual that counts, but only the future, which is made into a cruel divinity with absolute power over everyone and everything.

The collapse of the Communist systems was due in the first instance to their false economic dogmatics. But there is a tendency to overlook the deeper fact that they broke down because of their contempt for man and because they subordinated morality to the needs of the system and its promises of a glowing future. The real catastrophe that the Communist regimes left behind is not economic. It consists in the devastation of souls, in the destruction of moral consciousness. I see a fundamental contemporary problem for Europe and for the world in that while no one contests the economic failure, and former Communists do not hesitate to become economic liberals, there is an almost total silence about the moral and religious problems that were the real heart of the matter. And this means that the problems left behind by Marxism are still with us. The dissolution of the primal certainties of man about God, about himself, and about the universe — the dissolution of the consciousness of those moral values that are never subject to our own judgment — all this is still our problem. In a new form, it could lead to the self-destruction of European consciousness, and we must take this seriously as a real danger — independently of Spengler's vision of doom.[12]

WHERE DO WE STAND TODAY?

This brings us to the question: What is to happen now? In the tremendous upheavals of our age, is there an identity of Europe that has a future and to which we can sincerely commit ourselves? For the fathers of European unification after the devastations of the Second World War — Adenauer, Schumann, De Gasperi — it was clear that such a basis does exist and that it consists in the Christian patrimony of our continent, which owes its very existence to Christianity. They were

---

12. Here I should like to quote the words of E. Chargaff, *Ein zweites Leben: Autobiographische und andere Texte* (Stuttgart, 1995), 168: "Where everyone is free to pull the wool over the eyes of his neighbor as in the example of the free market economy, we end up with a 'Marsyas' society, a society of bleeding corpses."

certain that the devastations that confronted us in the Nazi dictatorship and in that of Stalin were due precisely to the rejection of this basis, thanks to a hubris that refused to submit to the Creator but claimed to have the power to create the better, "new" man and to remodel the bad world of the Creator into the good world proclaimed by the dogmatism of their own ideology. They were certain that these dictatorships, which had given birth to a wholly new quality of evil — much worse than all the horrors of the war — had their roots in the intention to abolish Europe and that it was necessary to return to that which had given its dignity to this continent despite all its sufferings and mistakes.

The initial enthusiasm for a return to the great constant elements of the Christian heritage soon evaporated, and European unification proceeded almost exclusively from the economic perspective. Scant attention was paid to the question of the *intellectual foundations* of such a community.

In recent years, people have become more aware that the economic fellowship of the European states also needs a basis in common values. The growth of violence, the escape into drugs, and the increase in corruption make it all too obvious that the decline of values has tangible material consequences and that we must do something to halt this. I do not wish to enter the discussion about the European constitution, the text of which is now available. All I wish to do is to mention three essential elements that must be included in the constitution if it is to do justice to the task of providing the moral foundations for the common European structures that are now taking shape. Europe needs these foundations, and they must be in tune with the great imperatives of its history.

The first element is the absoluteness that must be affirmed with regard to human dignity and human rights. This is antecedent to every law promulgated by the state. Günter Hirsch has rightly emphasized that these basic rights are neither created by the legislator nor bestowed on the citizens: "Rather, they exist in virtue of their own law, and the legislator is obliged a priori to respect them. They are higher values that the legislator must obey in his work."[13] This validity of human dignity, which comes before all political action and decision making, points ultimately to the Creator. It is only he who can posit laws that are rooted in the essence of man and that no one may alter. This means that an essential Christian inheritance is codified here in its own special form of validity. The fact that there exist values that no one may manipulate is the real guarantee of our freedom and of our human greatness. Faith sees therein the mystery of the Creator and of the divine likeness that he has bestowed on man. Hence, this proposition protects an essential element of the Christian identity of Europe in a formulation that even the nonbeliever can understand.

No one today would deny the priority of human dignity and of basic human rights over every political decision. The terrors of Nazism and of its racial doctrine are still too recent. But in the concrete sphere of so-called medical progress there are very real threats to these values. Who can fail to see the silent hollowing-out of human dignity entailed in cloning, in storing human fetuses for purposes of research and organ donation, or in the entire realm of genetical manipulation? To these we must add the increasing human trafficking that now threatens. Then come new forms of slavery and the trade in human organs for the purpose of transplantation. Naturally, a "good cause" is always presented in order to justify something that in fact cannot be justified.

Let us summarize: the legal enactment of the value and dignity of man, of freedom, equality, and solidarity, together with the fundamental principles of democracy and of the rule of law in society, entails an image of man, a moral option, and a concept of law that are not at all self-explanatory. These

---

13. G. Hirsch, "Ein Bekenntnis zu den Grundwerten," *Frankfurter allgemeine Zeitung*, October 12, 2000.

are, however, basic factors in Europe's identity, and they must be guaranteed, together with their direct consequences for public life. Naturally, all this can be defended only when a corresponding moral consciousness is developed anew.

Now I come to a second point for European identity: *marriage and the family*. Monogamous marriage, as the basic structure for the relationship between a man and a woman and as the cell for the construction of civic society, has been formed by biblical faith. It has given Europe — East and West — its specific "face" and its specifically human character, precisely because one must struggle again and again to realize the form of fidelity and of renunciation that monogamous marriage by its very nature requires. Europe would cease to be Europe if this basic cell of its social construction were to disappear or to be changed in its essence. We are all aware of the risks confronting marriage and the family today — partly because its indissolubility is watered down by an ever easier access to divorce, and partly because of the increasing cohabitation of men and women without the legal form of marriage.

The paradoxical modern demand of homosexual partnerships to receive a legal form that is more or less the equivalent of marriage is a clear antithesis to this tradition. This trend departs from the entire moral history of mankind, which — despite all the variety in the legal forms governing marriage — has always been aware that this is essentially a special form of the relationship of men and women, open to children and hence to the formation of a family. This is not a question of discrimination. Rather, we must ask what man is as man and as woman, and how we may correctly shape the relationship between them. If this relationship becomes increasingly detached from legal forms, while at the same time homosexual partnerships are increasingly viewed as equal in rank to marriage, we are on the verge of a dissolution of our concept of man, and the consequences can only be extremely grave. Unfortunately, the text of the constitution says nothing about this.

My last point concerns the religious sphere. Space does not permit me to discuss the large questions that are currently being debated here. I limit myself therefore to *one* point that is fundamental in all cultures, namely, reverence for that which is holy to other persons and reverence for the Holy One, God. One can certainly demand this even of those who are not themselves willing to believe in God. Where this reverence is shattered, something essential in a society perishes. We may be glad that one who mocks the faith of Israel, its image of God, or its great figures will be punished in today's society. The same is true of those who scorn the Koran and the basic convictions of Islam. When, however, it is a question of Christ and of that which Christians revere as holy, it appears that freedom of opinion is the highest good and that any limitation on this would endanger or even destroy tolerance and freedom as a whole. But freedom of opinion has an inherent limit: it is not entitled to destroy the honor and dignity of other persons, nor is it a freedom to utter lies or to destroy human rights. Here we may observe a strange self-hatred of the West that can only be called pathological. There is a praiseworthy openness that tries to understand foreign values, but all that one sees in one's own history is cruelty and destruction. We must also learn to see that which was great and pure.

If Europe is to survive, it needs a new acceptance of itself — naturally, a critical and humble acceptance. We hear passionate demands for multiculturalism, but this is sometimes primarily a refusal to accept that which is one's own or indeed a flight from that which is one's own. Without shared constants, without criteria rooted in that which is one's own, multiculturalism cannot endure. It surely cannot survive without reverence for that which is holy. This involves encountering with reverence that which is holy to another, but we can do this only if the Holy One, God himself, is not foreign to us.

Certainly we can and must learn from that which is holy to others, but it is our obligation both in relation to them and to our own selves to nourish our own reverence for the Holy One and to show the face of the God who has appeared to us, the God who cares for the poor and the weak, the widows and orphans and strangers, the God who is so human that he himself became one of us, a suffering man whose compassion with our suffering gives us dignity and hope. If we fail to do this, we are not only denying the identity of Europe; we are also depriving others of a service to which they are entitled. The absolutely profane character that has developed in the West is utterly alien to the cultures of the world, which are convinced that a world without God has no future. Hence it is precisely multiculturalism that summons us back to our own selves.

We do not know what the future holds in store for Europe. The charter of basic rights can be first a step to the renewed search for its soul. Toynbee was correct to maintain that the fate of a society always depends on creative minorities. Believing Christians ought to understand themselves as just such a creature minority and help Europe regain the best elements of its inheritance. This will allow Europe to serve the whole of mankind.

10

Common Identity and Common Will

Chances and Dangers for Europe

☙

What is Europe? What can and should it be in the total context of the historical movement in which we are involved at the beginning of the third Christian millennium? After the Second World War, the search for a common identity and a common will in Europe entered a new phase. After two suicidal wars had devastated Europe in the first half of the twentieth century and inflicted terrible suffering on the whole world, it had become clear that all the European states were the losers in this cruel drama and that everything must be done to prevent its recurrence.

INSTEAD OF DIVISIVE NATIONALISMS, ONE COMMON IDENTITY

Europe has always been a continent of contrasts, shaken to its core by many conflicts. In the nineteenth century the national states had come into being, and their competing interests had given a new dimension to destructive hostility. The work of European unification was guided basically by two motivations.

151

In response to the divisive nationalisms and the hegemonistic ideologies that had given the old hostilities a radical form in the Second World War, it was intended that the common cultural, moral, and religious inheritance of Europe should shape the awareness of its nations. This common identity of all the European peoples was to open up a path of peace, a path into the future that all could take together. The search was for a European identity that would not extinguish or deny the individual national identities but would bind them together in a higher fellowship to form one single community of peoples. The shared history was to be activated as a force for peace. There can be no doubt that the founding fathers of European unification regarded the Christian heritage as the core of this historical identity, though naturally not in its confessional forms. That which is common to all Christians, transcending denominational borders, seemed to them to supply a force strong enough to harmonize political conduct in the world. And this did not appear incompatible with the great moral impulses of the Enlightenment, which had displayed the rational side of Christianity, so to speak, and which seemed compatible with the essential impulses derived from the Christian history of Europe, despite all the antitheses that had existed in the past. This overarching conviction never completely clarified a number of individual points in the drama of the confessional divisions and in the battles fought by the pioneers of the Enlightenment, and this means that questions were left open that still await a proper examination. In the first phase of European unification, however, the conviction that the great building blocks of the European heritage were compatible was stronger than the questions that this process necessarily posed.

At the outset of European unification, a second motivation accompanied this historical and moral element. With the end of the Second World War, European dominance of the world, which had been expressed above all in the colonial system with its interlocking economic and political networks, had collapsed once and for all. In this sense, Europe as a whole had lost the war. America was now the dominant power on the stage of world history. But Japan, although defeated, also became an economic power alongside the United States, and the Soviet Union with its satellite states formed an *imperium* to which states in the Third World looked for support against America and Western Europe.

In this new situation, the individual European states could no longer act as equal partners with the superpowers. It was necessary to bind together their interests in one common European structure if Europe was to retain any importance at all in world politics. National interests had to be integrated into a common European interest. In addition to the search for a common identity generated by history that could promote peace, there was also the defense of common interests and therefore the intention to exercise that economic power which is a precondition of political power. In the course of the last fifty years, this second aspect of European unification has become ever more predominant. Indeed, it is this aspect alone that determines virtually every question. The euro, the common European currency, is the clearest expression of what the work of European unification means from this second perspective: Europe presents itself as an economic and monetary totality that as such takes part in shaping history and defends its own place.

Karl Marx maintained that religions and philosophies were merely ideological superstructures concealing the true realities of an economic situation. This is certainly not correct. One ought in fact to reverse this proposition and say that intellectual attitudes determine economic conduct and that economic situations then, in turn, have a decisive influence on religious and moral perspectives. After the initial phase in which ethical and religious considerations played a decisive role, economic considerations came to be the dominant factor in the development of Europe as an economic power.

SHARED CRITERIA FOR ACTION

Now, however, we can see with increasing clarity that the development of economic structures and activity go hand in hand with intellectual decisions. At first, very little explicit reflection on these decisions takes place, but they come to demand a greater measure of clarification. Great international conferences like those held in Cairo (1994) and Beijing (1995) articulate the search for shared criteria for action, but these are more than merely the expression of questions. One could call them a kind of council of the world spirit, at which shared certainties are formulated and declared to be normative for human existence. The policy of granting or withholding economic aid is one way of enforcing such norms, which deal primarily with the control of population growth in the world and the universal obligation to employ particular means to achieve this goal.

The old ethical norms governing the relationship between men and women took the form of tribal traditions in Africa. In the great Asiatic cultures, they were derived from the regulations of the cosmic order. In the monotheistic cultures, they were an appropriate application of the model supplied by the Ten Commandments. They are being replaced today by a system of norms that presupposes a total sexual freedom. At the same time, its primary concern is to lay down the maximum size for the world's population and to prescribe the technical means that must be made available. A similar tendency presides at the great conferences on world climate. In both cases, the search for norms is prompted by fear that world reserves will be pressed beyond their limits. In both cases, the participants desire to defend the freedom of human dealings with reality while also reducing the consequences of an unlimited exercise of this freedom.

The third type of large-scale international conferences, the summits at which the leading economic powers try to regulate the globalized economy, has become the ideological battlefield of the post-Communist period. On the one hand, technology and economics present themselves as vehicles that facilitate the radical freedom of man. On the other, their omnipresence, with their inherent norms, is now seen as a global dictatorship. And those who fight against this globalization employ an anarchic wildness that would almost suggest that they see the freedom to destroy as an essential part of human freedom as a whole.

THE TASK FACING US

What does all this mean for the question about Europe? It means that a construction that aimed one-sidedly at the consolidation of economic power is now giving birth to a new kind of system of values, and we must examine to what extent this will serve our needs in the present and the future. The European Charter that was recently published could be called an attempt to find a middle path between this new canon of values and the classical values of European tradition. It will certainly prove helpful as an initial indication of the direction to be taken, although ambiguities on important points make it impossible to overlook the problems inherent in this kind of attempt at mediation between differing perspectives. We must carry out an examination of the urgent questions on the level of basic principles, but it is obvious that space does not permit me to do this here. All I wish to do is to try to formulate more precisely the issue at stake.

As we have seen, the fathers of European unification in the aftermath of the Second World War agreed that there was a basic compatibility between the moral heritage of Christianity and the moral heritage of the European Enlightenment. In the Enlightenment, the idea of autonomous reason led to a transformation of the biblical concept of God in another direction: God the Creator and Sustainer, who continuously maintains and guides the world, had become merely the initiator who "kicked off" the universe. The concept of revelation was eliminated. In many ways, Spinoza's formula *Deus sive natura* ("God, or nature") can be called characteristic of the Enlightenment vision. But this means that there was indeed faith in a kind of nature that bore the divine imprint and in the capacity of man to understand this nature and to evaluate it as making a rational claim upon him.

Marxism made a radical break with this faith. The world that exists is a product of evolution in which reason plays no role, and it is only man who can bring forth the rational world from the irrational raw material of reality. This, united to Hegel's philosophy of history, to the liberal dogma of progress, and to the socioeconomic interpretation generated by this dogma, led to the expectation of a classless society that would appear in the course of historical progress as the final product of the class struggle. This became ultimately the only normative moral idea: whatever serves to bring closer this state of salvation is good, and whatever opposes it is evil. Today, a second Enlightenment has not only moved on from the *Deus sive natura* but has also seen through the irrationality of the Marxist ideology of hope. Instead of this, it postulates a rational future goal that bears the title "new world order" and is now meant to become the basic ethical norm. It shares with Marxism the evolutionistic idea that the world we encounter is the product of irrational chance and of its own inherent regular processes, which means that the world cannot bear any ethical directives in itself as the old idea of nature envisaged. The attempt to deduce rules for human conduct from the rules of evolution is widespread, but scarcely convincing. An increasing number of philosophers, such as Singer, Rorty, and Sloterdijk, are raising their voices to tell us that man has the right and the duty to construct the world anew in a rational manner. Hardly anyone questions the need for a new world order, which must be a world order of rationality. So far, so good. But what is "rational"?

The criterion of rationality is taken exclusively from the experience of technological production based on science. Rationality is oriented to functionality, to effectiveness, and to an increase in the quality of life for all. This entails a use — indeed a domination — of nature that is problematic in view of the dramatic environmental problems our world now faces. But man's domination of his own self nonchalantly takes ever greater steps toward the realization of Aldous Huxley's vision. Man is no longer to be born in an irrational manner but it to be produced rationally. Man as a product is subject to the control of man. Imperfect individuals must be weeded out; the path of planning and production must aim at the perfect man. Suffering must disappear, and life is to consist of pleasure alone.

Such radical visions remain rare and are mostly presented in milder forms. But more and more people agree with the maxim for conduct that says that man is permitted to do whatever he is able to do. When the world is understood in evolutionary terms, it is obvious that there cannot be absolute values; nothing is always bad, and nothing is always good. The only way to discern moral norms is to evaluate the various goods involved in a particular question. This, however, means that higher goals, such as the expectation of success in curing diseases, would justify even the abuse of man, provided only that the good one hopes for appears sufficiently great.

This leads to new forms of coercion and the emergence of a new ruling class. In the final analysis, it is those who possess the professional know-how and those who control the purse strings and the technical equipment who decide the fate of others. When scientists are told that they must not let their competitors get ahead of them in research, this itself becomes a coercive force from which there is no escape, and this coercion now dictates the direction of scientific research. In this situation, what advice can one give Europe and the world? The departure from every ethical tradition and the insistence that all that counts is technological rationality and the possibilities it opens up to us appears specifically European in this situation. But will not a world order with such foundations turn out to be a utopia of terror? Does not Europe — does not the world — need corrective elements drawn from its own tradition and from the great ethical traditions of mankind?

The inviolability of man ought to be an unassailed pillar of ethical regulations. We cannot trust one another and live together in peace unless man recognizes that he is an ultimate end, not a means to some other end, and unless we consequently regard other persons as sacred and inviolable. There is no evaluation of goods that could justify treating man as experimental material for higher purposes. We act ethically — not on the basis of calculations — only when we see this as an absolute principle that stands higher than all evaluations of goods. The inviolability of human dignity also entails that this dignity belongs to every man, to each individual who has a human face and belongs biologically to the human species. Functional criteria cannot possess any validity here: the suffering, handicapped, or unborn human being is a human being. I should like to add that this must be linked to respect for the origin of man in the sexual union of man and woman: man may not become a product. He may not be produced, but only begotten. And this is why one of the constant elements of every humane society is the protection of the special dignity of the fellowship of man and woman on which the future of the human race depends.

All this is possible only if we acquire a new sensitivity to the dignity of suffering. Learning to live also means learning to suffer. This is why reverence for that which is holy is also essential. Faith in the Creator God is the surest guarantee of human dignity. Faith cannot be imposed on anyone, but since it represents a great good for society, it is entitled to claim reverence even on the part of nonbelievers.

It is correct to affirm that rationality is a basic characteristic of the European spirit, thanks to which this spirit has conquered the world — for it is the form of rationality that first emerged in Europe that influences life on all the continents today. But this rationality can turn destructive if it cuts itself off from its roots and makes technological ability the only criterion of conduct. It is vital that it remain connected to the two great sources of knowledge, nature and history. Neither realm simply imparts information, but both can suggest directions. Nature resists unbridled consumption, and this is why the state of the environment has prompted new reflections on the direction that nature itself indicates. The lordship over nature of which the biblical Creation narrative speaks does not mean a violent exploitation of nature but rather an understanding of nature's inherent possibilities. This suggests a caution in the way in which we serve nature and nature serves us.

The beginning of human life is both a natural and a human process. In the sexual union of man and woman, the natural and the intellectual elements unite to form that which is specifically human, and one ignores this at one's peril. The historical experiences of man, which have been reflected in the great religions, are an abiding source of knowledge and provide directives for reason that apply even to those who do not identify with any one of these traditions. The attempt to think and to live without any contact with these great traditions would be an arrogance that ultimately leaves man helpless and empty.

My remarks do not amount to a conclusive answer to the question of the foundations on which Europe is to be built. All I have sought to do is to sketch the task that faces us. We must not delay in getting to work on it.

Epilogue

Belief in the Triune God and Peace in the World

❧

Not Threat, but Rescue

The feast of the Most Holy Trinity is unlike the other great feasts of the Church's year, such as Christmas, Epiphany, Easter, or Pentecost. On those days, we celebrate God's mighty deeds in history: his Incarnation, his Resurrection, the sending of the Spirit and, with that, the birth of the Church. On the feast of the Trinity, we are not celebrating one of the events by which something of God becomes visible to us. We are quite simply celebrating God himself. We rejoice that God exists, and we give thanks that he is as he is and that we are permitted to know him and love him because he himself knows us, loves us, and has shown himself to us. But is the existence of God, his being, and the fact that we are known by God truly a reason for joy? This is not something that can be taken for granted.

Many deities of the world religions are terrifying, cruel, egoistic, or impenetrable, a mixture of good and evil. Many in the ancient world were frightened of the gods and of their sinister power: one must try to win them over; one must endeavor to escape from their terrible moods. One element in the redemptive force of the Christian mission was its dismissal of the entire world of the gods as a mere outward show, while it presented the one God who has become man in Jesus Christ, the God who is reason and love, the God who is stronger than all the dark powers that may exist in the world. Paul said, "We know that 'an idol has no real existence,' and that 'there is no God but one.' " He continued: "For although there may be so-called gods in heaven or on earth — and indeed there are many 'gods' and many 'lords' — yet for us there is one God, the Father" (1 Cor. 8:5–6). Even today, this message brings about a redemptive revolution in those regions where the old tribal religions hold sway: one need not cower in fear at every turn before the spirits who surround one and whom one repeatedly tries in vain to banish. "He who dwells in the shelter of the Most High, who abides in the shadow of the Almighty" (Ps. 91:1), knows that he is truly safe. One who knows the God of Jesus Christ knows that all those other forms of fear of God that are now spreading afresh in our world, the destructive existential fear, have been overcome once and for all.

In view of all the terrible things in our world, many people are moved to ask: Does God exist? Where is he? And if he does exist, is he truly good? Is he not rather a sinister God or even dangerous? This question has taken a new form in the modern period. God's existence looks like a limitation of our freedom. Someone is watching us; his eyes follow our every step. The rebellion against God in the modern period is generated by the fear that is induced by the omnipresent eye of God, which seems threatening. We do not want be seen; we just want to be ourselves. Man feels truly free, truly himself, only when he has got rid of God. We find this already in the story of Adam, who regards God as a competitor. Adam wants to be the author of his own life; he hides from God "among the trees of the garden" (Gen. 3:8). Sartre once said that one would have to deny the existence of God, even if he in fact existed, since the very idea of God contradicts the freedom and greatness of man.

But has the world become brighter, happier, or freer since it got rid of God? Has not this stripped man of his dignity, damning him to an empty freedom in which he is ready to do any kind of cruelty? God's eye is frightening only when one regards this as dependence and servitude instead of recognizing that the love expressed in his eyes is that which makes our existence possible, that which allows us to live. "He who has seen me has seen the Father," says the Lord to Philip and to all of us (John 14:9). The face of Jesus is the face of God. That is what God looks like. Jesus, who suffered for us and forgave his enemies while dying on the cross, shows us how God is. This eye does not threaten us: it rescues us.

Yes, we are entitled to rejoice that God exists, that he has shown himself to us, and that he never leaves us alone. It is a comfort to know the telephone numbers of friends and good people; this means that they are never very far away from us, never completely absent. We can phone them, and they can phone us. God's incarnation in Christ tells us that God has written our names in his address book, so to speak. We can call him, without needing money or technology. He is always within reach of our voices. Thanks to baptism and confirmation, we belong to his family, and he is always on the line: "I am with you always, to the close of the age" (Matt. 28:20).

THE PROMISE

Today's Gospel adds another important affirmation. Jesus promises the Spirit of truth (John 16:13), and he gives him the name "Paraclete" several times in the course of the same discourse. What does this mean? In Latin, this word was translated *consolator*, often rendered in English as "comforter." This Latin noun, interpreted very literally, means the one who enters our solitude and shares it, the one who is with us in

our solitude so that this ceases to be solitude. Solitude is a
sphere of sadness for man because he needs love. A solitude
that is not lit up by any ray of love, a solitude that follows
on the loss of love, threatens the innermost condition of our
life. Being unloved is the core of human suffering and human
sadness. The word *consolator* tells us we are never completely
alone, never completely abandoned by love. Through the Holy
Spirit, God has entered our solitude, and he opens a breach
in its wall. This is the true consolation, not only a consolation in words, but a consolation in the power of reality. In
the Middle Ages, this name of the Holy Spirit suggested that
man too is obliged to enter into the solitude of those who
suffer, and this is why hospices for the elderly were dedi-
cated to the Holy Spirit. Thus, men were charged to carry
out the work of the Holy Spirit, to be comforters who entered the solitude of sufferers and the elderly and brought
them light. What a task this represents for us all today in our
own world!

The Greek word *paraklêtos* can also be translated in another way: it means "advocate," and we can see what this
means if we look at Revelation 12:10: "Now the salvation
and the power and the kingdom . . . have come, for the accuser
of our brethren has been thrown down, who accuses them day
and night before our God." One who does not love God does
not love human beings either. Those who deny God very soon
turn to slandering his Creation and start leveling accusations
at others, for it is ultimately only by means of accusations
against Creation and man that they can justify their hostility
toward God. Their logic asserts that the God who made all
this is not good. The Holy Spirit, the Spirit of God, is not
the accuser but the defender of man and Creation. God himself pleads on behalf of his creature, man. God defends his
own self in his Creation, and he also defends us. God is on
our side: this became clearly visible in every step of the path

taken by Jesus, whose whole life was a pleading on our behalf, even unto death. This insight leads Paul to cry out in joy:
"If God is for us, who is against us? ... Who shall bring any
charge against God's elect? It is God who justifies; who is to
condemn? Is it Christ Jesus, who died, yes, who was raised
from the dead, who is at the right hand of God, who indeed
intercedes for us? ... For I am sure that neither death nor life,
nor angels nor principalities, nor things present nor things to
come, nor powers, nor height, nor depth, nor anything else in
all creation, will be able to separate us from the love of God
in Christ Jesus our Lord" (Rom. 8:31–39).

We rejoice in this God and we celebrate him. To know him
and to profess faith in him is immensely important today. In
these days we recall the horrors of the Second World War and
give thanks that Hitler's dictatorship with all its cruelties was
swept away and that Europe regained its freedom. But we cannot overlook the fact that today's world too is full of cruelties
and threats. Abuse of the image of God, man, is just as dangerous as that denial of God which was proclaimed so loudly
in the ideologies of the twentieth century and in the totalitarian regimes which propagated these ideologies and laid waste
the world both externally and internally, even in the depths of
souls. Today, at this precise hour in history, Europe and the
world need the presence of the God who has revealed himself in Jesus Christ and remains close to us in the Holy Spirit.
As Christians, we are responsible for maintaining the presence
of God in our world, for it is only this presence that has the
power to keep man from destroying himself.

TRIUNE LOVE

God is three, and God is one: he is not eternal solitude but
the eternal love that is the basis of the relationships between
the three Persons and the foundation of all being and life. The
unity that this love creates — the Trinitarian unity — is a higher

unity than the unity of the building blocks of matter that are indivisible on their lowest level. There is nothing rigid in the highest unity: it is love. The most beautiful picture of this mystery was given us by Andrei Rublev in the fifteenth century in his celebrated icon of the Trinity. It does not portray the eternal mystery of God in his own self, for who would dare do that? It shows this mystery mirrored in a historical event, the visit of three men to Abraham near the oaks of Mamre (Gen. 18:1–33). Abraham soon realizes that these are not ordinary men and that in them God himself is visiting him. Even in the Old Testament text, the number three forms a mysterious bridge into the oneness of God: there are three of them, in whom Abraham adores the One, and this enabled Christians to see this narrative as a mirror of the Trinity from an early date. Rublev's icon makes the many dimensions of this mysterious event wonderfully clear but preserves its mysterious character while doing so.

I should like to mention only one trait in this rich icon, namely, the surroundings of the event, which also help express the mystery of the Persons. First, we see the oaks of Mamre, which Rublev gathers into one single tree, which now portrays the tree of life — the tree of life that consists in nothing other than the triune love that created the world, sustains it and redeems it, and is the source of all life. Then we see the tent, Abraham's house, which reminds us of John 1:14: "The Word became flesh and dwelt [set up his tent] among us.... " The body of the incarnate God has itself become the tent, the house, in which God dwells and in which God becomes our dwelling, our resting place. Lastly, we see Abraham's gift: the "calf, tender and good" of Genesis is replaced here by the chalice, the sign of the Eucharist, the sign of that gift in which God bestows himself: "Love, sacrifice, immolation precede the act of the creation of the world, and are the source of this act."[1]

---

1. P. Evdokimov, *L'art de l'icône: Théologie de la Beauté* (Paris, 1970), 208.

The tree — the tent — the chalice. They show us the mystery of God; they allow us as it were to look into his heart, into the triune love. It is this God that we celebrate. It is in this God that we rejoice. He is the true hope of our world. Amen.

Note on First Publication
of the Essays in This Book

ༀ

Part I
WHAT RULES SHOULD
GUIDE OUR CONDUCT?
Politics and Morality

Chapter 1
To Change or to Preserve?
Political Visions and Political Praxis

"Politische Vision und Praxis der Politik," lecture in Trent, September 20, 2002. First published in Italian in Joseph Ratzinger, *Europa: I suoi fondamenti oggi e domani* (Cinisello Balsamo: Edizioni San Paolo, 2004), 43–59.

Chapter 2
What Keeps the World Together
The Prepolitical Moral Foundations of a Free State

"Was die Welt zusammenhält: Vorpolitische moralische Grundlagen eines freiheitlichen Staates," contribution to a debate at the Catholic Academy in Bavaria, January 19, 2004.

Chapter 3
FREEDOM, LAW, AND THE GOOD
Moral Principles in Democratic Societies

"Die Freiheit, das Recht und das Gute: Moralische Prinzipien in demokratischen Gesellschaften," an address delivered when the author was made an associate foreign member of the Académie des Sciences Morales et Politiques of the Institut de France on November 7, 1992; the notes were added for publication in the present book. First publication: *Wahrheit, Werte, Macht: Prüfsteine der pluralistischen Gesellschaft*, 3rd ed. (Freiburg i.Br., 1995), 11–24.

Chapter 4
WHAT IS TRUTH?
The Significance of Religious and Ethical Values in a Pluralistic Society

"Die Bedeutung religiöser und sittlicher Werte in der pluralistischen Gesellschaft," *Internationale katholische Zeitschrift "Communio"* 21, no. 6 (1992): 500–512; republished in *Wahrheit, Werte, Macht* (see above), 63–92.

Part II
RESPONSIBILITY FOR PEACE
Orientations

Chapter 5
IF YOU WANT PEACE . . .
Conscience and Truth

"Wenn du Frieden willst, achte das Gewissen jedes Menschen: Gewissen und Wahrheit," in *Fides quaerens intellectum: Beiträge zur Fundamentaltheologie*, ed. Michael Kessler, Wolfhart Pannenberg, and Hermann Josef Pottmeyer (Tübingen: Francke Verlag, 1992); slightly abbreviated; first published in full in *Wahrheit, Werte, Macht* (see above), 27–62.

Chapter 6
SEARCHING FOR PEACE
Tensions and Dangers

"Auf der Suche nach dem Frieden," an address given on the sixtieth anniversary of the landing of the Allies in France, June 6, 2004; first published in the newspaper *Die Tagespost*, June 12, 2004, 4–5.

Chapter 7
WHAT MUST WE DO?
Christians' Responsibility for Peace

"Die Verantwortung der Christen für den Frieden," an address during the ecumenical celebration in the cathedral of Bayeux on June 6, 2004; first published in German in *Die Tagespost*, June 15, 2004, 6.

Chapter 8
ACTING IN THE STRENGTH THAT COMES FROM REMEMBRANCE
The Grace of Reconciliation

"Gnade der Versöhnung," an address held in the German cemetery at La Cambe near Caen, France, June 5, 2004; first published in *Die Tagespost*, June 15, 2004, 6.

Part III
WHAT IS EUROPE?
Foundations and Perspectives

Chapter 9
EUROPE'S IDENTITY
Its Intellectual Foundations Yesterday, Today, and Tomorrow

"Europas Identität: Seine geistigen Grundlagen gestern, heute, morgen," a lecture in the Italian Senate in Rome, May 13, 2004; first published in Italian in Joseph Ratzinger, *Europa: I suoi fondamenti* (see above), 9–29; also in Joseph Ratzinger and Marcello Pera, *Senza radici: Europa, relativismo, Cristianesimo* (Rome: Islam Mondadori, 2004), 47–72.

Chapter 10
COMMON IDENTITY AND COMMON WILL
Chances and Dangers for Europe

"Chancen und Gefahren für Europa," a lecture to economic experts and politicians in Cernobbio (Como) on September 8, 2001. The limit of twenty minutes meant that it was possible to show only that the questions connected with Europe cannot be reduced to the political and economic dimension. Time did not permit me to go beyond the illustration of the problem and suggest paths to a solution.

EPILOGUE
Belief in the Triune God and Peace in the World

"Der Glaube an den dreifaltigen Gott und der Friede in der Welt," a sermon on the feast of the Holy Trinity on June 6, 2004, in the cathedral of Bayeux on the occasion of the commemorative celebrations in Caen of the sixtieth anniversary of the landing of the Allies in Normandy on June 6, 1944; first published in German in *Die Tagespost*, June 12, 2004, 3.